"There's simply no one like Lisa Harper. In *A Jesus-Shaped Life*, she bridges the gap between sound doctrine and a flourishing life. She makes theology both accessible and desirable for all, inspiring us to receive the unconditional love of our merciful and gracious Savior. You will laugh, cry, be challenged, and be compelled to lean in more fully to a Jesus-shaped life."

Christine Caine, founder of A21 and Propel Women

"Like the Master Storyteller, Lisa Harper knows how to draw you in through stories. She talks about theology in a way anybody can relate to. As you would expect if you've heard or read Lisa before, this book is like a conversation. But more than that, it's an invitation into deeper conversation—about, and especially with, God Himself."

Dr. Craig S. Keener, FM and Ada Thompson Professor of Biblical Studies at Asbury Theological Seminary

"Lisa's wit and humor are well known throughout the Christian world. Her ability to bring the Bible to life in unique and life-giving ways has always been her trademark. And now she combines those gifts to bring us a very readable and enjoyable work on our core Christian theological beliefs. Everyone should buy this book. Pick it up, grab a cup of coffee, and devour it!"

Dr. Jim Howard, professor in the Doctor of Ministry program at Denver Seminary, senior pastor at Dillon Community Church, and cohost of the *Back Porch Theology* podcast

"I can tell you from experience that sitting on an actual back porch with Lisa Harper is the best way to learn theology from her, preferably after you have laughed until you cried and eaten enough chips and guac to bust the top button on your denim—but this book is the next best thing! My big sister has never gotten over the grace of God. From the vantage point she loves best, on her knees at the feet of her Savior, she will help you discover the way to a Jesus-shaped life, and you will never be the same."

Levi Lusko, author of *Blessed Are the Spiraling: How the Chaotic Search for Significance Can Lead to Joy Through Life's Shifting Seasons*

"When you see a book about theology, it may scare you away or maybe intimidate you because you don't feel like you're smart enough to understand it. However, in *A Jesus-Shaped Life*, we learn that sound biblical theology makes us more Christlike and gives us a road map for how we should live."

Sadie Robertson Huff, author, speaker, and founder of Live Original

"Lisa Harper shows us how theology is supposed to work: She takes her personal experiences of pain and loss and her questions of doubt and shame and holds them up to the light of Scripture. In *A Jesus-Shaped Life*, her signature humor and deep empathy blend with clear theological truths: God loves us, pursues us, and forgives us, always and forever. Grab a coffee and settle in for a theology lesson like you've never had before—real-life tested and fearlessly faithful to God the Father, Son, and Holy Spirit."

Lynn H. Cohick, PhD, Distinguished Professor of New Testament at Houston Christian University

A Jesus-Shaped Life

A Jesus-Shaped Life

How Diving Deeper into Theology Can Transform Us and Our World with the Radical Kindness of God

Lisa Harper

Revell

a division of Baker Publishing Group
Grand Rapids, Michigan

© 2025 by Lisa Harper

Published by Revell
a division of Baker Publishing Group
Grand Rapids, Michigan
RevellBooks.com

Printed in the United States of America

All rights reserved. No part of this publication may be reproduced, stored in a retrieval system, or transmitted in any form or by any means—for example, electronic, photocopy, recording—without the prior written permission of the publisher. The only exception is brief quotations in printed reviews.

Library of Congress Cataloging-in-Publication Data
Names: Harper, Lisa, 1963– author.
Title: A Jesus-shaped life : how diving deeper into theology can transform us and our world with the radical kindness of God / Lisa Harper.
Description: Grand Rapids, Michigan : Revell, a division of Baker Publishing Group, [2025] | Includes bibliographical references.
Identifiers: LCCN 2024041609 | ISBN 9780800744762 (cloth) | ISBN 9780800747725 (ITPE) | ISBN 9781493448555 (ebook)
Subjects: LCSH: Theology, Practical. | Christian life.
Classification: LCC BV3 .H335 2025 | DDC 230—dc23/eng/20241113
LC record available at https://lccn.loc.gov/2024041609

Unless otherwise indicated, Scripture quotations are from the Holy Bible, New International Version®, NIV®. Copyright © 1973, 1978, 1984, 2011 by Biblica, Inc.® Used by permission of Zondervan. All rights reserved worldwide. www.zondervan.com. The "NIV" and "New International Version" are trademarks registered in the United States Patent and Trademark Office by Biblica, Inc.®

Scripture quotations labeled CSB are from the Christian Standard Bible®. Copyright © 2017 by Holman Bible Publishers. Used by permission. Christian Standard Bible® and CSB® are federally registered trademarks of Holman Bible Publishers.

Scripture quotations labeled ESV are from The Holy Bible, English Standard Version® (ESV®). Copyright © 2001 by Crossway, a publishing ministry of Good News Publishers. Used by permission. All rights reserved. ESV Text Edition: 2016

Scripture quotations labeled KJV are from the King James Version of the Bible.

Scripture quotations labeled MSG are from *The Message*. Copyright © 1993, 2002, 2018 by Eugene H. Peterson. Used by permission of NavPress. All rights reserved. Represented by Tyndale House Publishers.

Scripture quotations labeled NCV are from the New Century Version®. Copyright © 2005 by Thomas Nelson. Used by permission. All rights reserved.

Scripture quotations labeled NLT are from the *Holy Bible*, New Living Translation. Copyright © 1996, 2004, 2015 by Tyndale House Foundation. Used by permission of Tyndale House Publishers, Carol Stream, Illinois 60188. All rights reserved.

Scripture quotations labeled RSV are from the Revised Standard Version of the Bible. Copyright © 1946, 1952, and 1971 National Council of the Churches of Christ in the United States of America. Used by permission. All rights reserved worldwide.

The quotation on page 171 and the epigraph in chapter 10 are from *Mere Christianity* by C. S. Lewis, copyright © 1942, 1943, 1944, 1952 C.S. Lewis Pte. Ltd. Extracts reprinted by permission.

Cover design by Laura Klynstra

Some names and details of people and situations described in this book have been changed or presented in composite form in order to ensure the privacy of those involved.

The author is represented by Alive Literary Agency, www.aliveliterary.com.

Baker Publishing Group publications use paper produced from sustainable forestry practices and postconsumer waste whenever possible.

This book is dedicated
to my dear friend of many years,
Allison Allen,
and to my spiritual mentor of many years as well
(because it's taking me longer than most of his students
at Denver Seminary to finish my doctorate),
Dr. Jim Howard.

Both of these saints have also become beloved cohorts and coconspirators on a podcast called *Back Porch Theology*. And I'd be remiss if I didn't include Rahny Taylor, our podcasting boss and tireless advocate, in this emotive dedication. Because Rahny took a huge risk in putting our motley crew on the air—he actually believed us when we told him that deep, biblical theology and copious belly laughs don't have to be mutually exclusive!

Contents

Foreword by Scot McKnight   11

Introduction   15

1. Theology Is Meant to Be Lived   19
2. Our God Is a Perfect "Us"   41
3. The Compassionate Authority of King Jesus   63
4. As Close as Your Next Breath   81
5. The Calibration of Christlikeness   101
6. The Odyssey to Theodicy   123
7. Our Family Resemblance   145
8. Christianity Is More *We* than *Me*   167
9. The Score Has Already Been Settled   189
10. The Embodiment of Theology   211

Acknowledgments   233

Foreword

Somewhere early in the book in your hands, my friend (whom I admire because of her love of Christ and whom my wife, Kris, loves—and Lisa likes her more than me, but I digress) Lisa Harper writes a stunning sentence: "Biblical *orthodoxy* (what we believe to be true of God) must lead to Christoformic *orthopraxy* (how we live in light of what we believe to be true of God)." You can tell she's been to seminary, can't you? So have I, so I liked her sentence and graded it with "Exquisite!" And at times my students write sentences just like that, and they are just as proud of themselves as Lisa and I are of ourselves.

Here's the problem. Lisa's perfectly manicured sentence above is a great idea until, like the good idea about the importance of forgiving others, you have to look at the face in the mirror to see if it looks like Jesus. If it doesn't, and I'm pretty sure it doesn't (at least once a day, or in my case, three times a day), then we need to take to heart that theology is meant to be lived. Lisa is right: Biblical orthodoxy is supposed to lead to Christlike orthopraxy. (I slightly adjusted Lisa's wonderful term *Christoformic*.)

I want to turn this around or upside down, and I ask you to consider this next statement. At some level, our biblical orthodoxy is actually Christoformic orthopraxy turned into theological theory and abstractions. Think about orthodoxy as the best ideas at work in a Jesus-shaped life, and you have what I am trying to say. Lisa's wonderful book ties both sides of these statements into a single whole. I'll give an example. I wrote a book called *The Jesus Creed* about Jesus's teaching, and that book contends that Jesus wanted us to practice the ancient Jewish Shema ("Hear, O Israel . . ."—found in Deuteronomy 6) and a commandment He tied to it, found in Leviticus, that instructs us to love our neighbor as ourselves. What a wonderful creed to live by, which is why I called the book *The Jesus Creed*. (I won't bother you now with how I tricked my editor into that becoming the title, but I really did.) So, the book has a good idea: The Christian life is about loving God and loving others (and loving ourselves). The trick is living it. One day I said something a bit un-Jesus-Creed-like to Lisa's friend, my wife, Kris. Kris said, "That wasn't very Jesus-Creed-like." I agreed but decided not to say much or I'd have to apologize. So I waited. A couple of weeks later, Kris said something a bit—well, for her—strong to me, so I piped up with a good one: "That wasn't very Jesus-Creed-like." Her response slayed me: "I didn't write that book."

Now, that's an illustration of what you will encounter in this book. But that little story I tell about myself is better than an illustration. I was held to the ideas of the Jesus Creed more intensively because I had written about how central and important and vital . . . and other good words . . . the Jesus Creed was. I had some solid biblical orthodoxy, but orthodoxy without orthopraxy is, to use the words of Jesus's brother, James, plain ol' dead faith. What good is faith if you don't practice it? James asked his audience. The answer—and you can almost hear the echoes from the first century—was "No good. No good." (Sing that to the tune of a Neil Diamond song, and you can get the room swinging arms and bobbing.) Orthodoxy and orthopraxy, for Jesus, are tied so closely together that separating them ruins both.

Lisa's book explores, like a piece of music that continues to deepen and widen with more and more instruments coming into play, what a Jesus-shaped life looks like. We need to learn about this because we are not Jesus, Jesus is not us, and when we give Jesus just a fair examination, we discover very quickly that we've got a long way to go. The deeper we go into the Jesus-shaped life, the more we realize that Jesus is simply unfathomable, and the irony is that His unfathomability draws us to Him in ways we would never expect.

Lisa's *Jesus-Shaped Life*, from her opening story about taking her beautiful daughter, Missy, to school with a little cream cheese on her perfectly pressed blouse to the very end of the book, reminds us all that theological education that does not lead to spiritual formation is not what God wants. "No good, no good." Sing it. Say it. Live it.

Scot McKnight

Introduction

As I'm writing this introduction, someone I love very much has just been moved into hospice care, and his neuro-oncologist has informed us that his death is imminent, within the next few hours or days. If you've experienced what seems to be an untimely death of someone you love, you've probably grappled with some of the same questions I have: *Why didn't this show up on earlier scans? Why didn't that experimental drug work? Why is such a good man having to navigate such a hard death? God, why are You letting him die now when his family needs him?* When life doesn't turn out the way we planned or prayed, emotional wrestling often follows.

The older I get, the more grateful I am that we have a Creator Redeemer who isn't disappointed or dishonored by our honest tussling. Instead, He invites us to bring *everything* to Him—our delight and despair and gladness and grieving. And He doesn't just "allow" us to ask questions; He effectively leans down and inclines His ear to listen (Ps. 116:2), whether we're lauding His greatness or listing our pain and disappointment. The King of all kings is not a faraway deity, ruling over the earth as we know it like a dispassionate, iron-fisted autocrat. *He is a relational God,* who deigns to make Himself knowable! Who loves us more than we can possibly ask or imagine. Who through His inscripturated Word and Holy Spirit is always beckoning us to come closer. While I labored to fill this book with sound biblical content and theological truisms (I sacrificed a lot of blood, sweat, tears, and cold, hard cash getting my doctorate at Denver Seminary, y'all, and I'll be darned if I'm not going to use a few of those big words I memorized!), it's not an academic tome as much as it is an encouragement to live life in lockstep with the Lover of your soul because accruing information *about* God pales next to experiencing intimacy *with* Jesus. That's why I've formatted the chapters in such a way that we can engage our minds with the cognitive information *and* engage our hearts with some practical ways to internalize and embody truths about who God is and who He's called us to be as His image bearers.

I've been a follower of Jesus Christ for more than fifty years now, as well as a vocational minister for almost forty years, and in my experience it's only when Christ followers develop real intimacy with Jesus that our stories resonate with the beautiful, broken world around us. Lost and lonely people are rightly repelled by religiosity. But they are compelled by genuine kindness. By Christians who at least faintly resemble the One they profess to follow. The most Christlike believers I've had the privilege of doing life with—the saints who walk what they talk and have grown into means of grace God is using to impact the world for His kingdom purposes—aren't necessarily the most knowledgeable; they're the ones who've spent the most time lingering in His embrace.

Thank you so much for your generous willingness to even pick this book up. If you find yourself reading a chapter or two or three, my huge hope and fervent prayer is that your heart will shift a bit closer toward Jesus with every turn of the page.

Gratefully,
Lisa

ONE

Theology Is Meant to Be Lived

> For millions of Christians, God is no more real than He is to non-Christians. They go through life trying to love an ideal and be loyal to a mere principle.
>
> A. W. Tozer

I have a confession to make. I've never worn a WWJD band around my wrist. Even in the nineties, when they first became popular, I never donned one. I understand admitting my aversion to those spiritually themed fashion accessories may come as a bit of a shock, but I have an aversion to how they tend to soak up dirt, body oil, and grime and become discolored and odiferous.

In fact, if you're wearing a WWJD or friendship bracelet right now—maybe it's a nostalgic reminder of a meaningful mission trip, or your adolescent daughter gave it to you in a rush of affection when she found out you bought her and her bestie tickets to a Taylor Swift concert—go ahead and lift your wrist to your nose and tell me I'm wrong. It's surprisingly offensive, isn't it? Which is the main reason I never jumped on the WWJD bracelet bandwagon. But I've often regretted the persnickety choice not to wear a tangible WHAT WOULD JESUS DO? memory aid because I regularly need to be reminded of how our Savior would've responded in situations where I don't remotely resemble Him!

I experienced fresh regret recently while driving my daughter Missy to school. She's normally a really, really sweet kid (I brought her home from Haiti through the miracle of adoption in 2014, and most days still find me in the honeymoon stage of parenting), but she is most certainly not a morning person, and unfortunately for her, I am. Suffice it to say, a sleepy seventh grader with surging hormones and a chatty middle-aged mother with perky intonations are a train wreck waiting to happen. Here's how that morning played out:

> Me (with positivity, albeit in a too-high-pitched voice): *Honey, why don't you go ahead and start eating your bagel because we've only got another ten minutes before we get to school, and remember your lunch period is pretty late this year, so you're going to be really hungry by math if you don't go ahead and eat some breakfast.*
>
> Missy (turns her head to look out the passenger's window but not before I recognize an exasperated eye roll): *Harrumph.*

Ninety seconds pass while lovely Lauren Daigle lyrics echo through the heavy silence in the car.

> Me (with intentionally lower-pitched positivity): *Hey Miss, honey, I know you would rather have a sausage biscuit this morning, but we didn't have time to stop at Huff's, so why don't you go ahead and start eating your bagel, okay?*
>
> Missy (remains fixated by the scenery outside her window but emits a heavy sigh): *Pfeuuuuuu.*

Two minutes pass, and Brooke Ligertwood lyrics extolling the name of Jesus begin reverberating through the emotional impasse in the car. A still, small voice in my head reminds me that companionable silence can be a very effective peace offering between mothers and teen daughters. But after waiting another long moment or two, I kick that proverbial petite voice in the shins and open my big mouth anyway.

> Me (with forced, mostly fake positivity): *Hey Babe, we're only a few minutes away from school, and the cream cheese on your bagel has started to melt now, so when you do take a bite, will you please lean forward and hold it over your paper plate so it doesn't drip all over your uniform?*

Mind you, her shirt was navy blue, and I'd ironed it perfectly that morning after starching her khaki pants with a beautiful, standing seam because, well, you know, I'm one of the oldest and one of the few single parents at her Christian school, so I'm passionate about making sure her uniform is on point to compensate. Unlike most of the other (and much younger!) middle school moms, I'm rarely wearing makeup, much less a matching Lululemon outfit, when we come barreling into the school parking lot mere minutes before her first class begins in the morning. Instead, I tend to be a sweatshirt-and-pajama-pants-with-her-hair-shoved-into-a-ball-cap kind of drop-off parent! I also don't bring homemade treats to class parties because, due to my work and travel schedule, our gleaming stainless-steel double oven functions mostly as kitchen art. Therefore, a guilt-ridden mom's gotta do what a guilt-ridden mom's gotta do, right? And that morning, it meant making sure my miracle child's outfit was as immaculate as a military cadet at roll call!

However, when another minute passed and I glanced over to gauge Missy's bagel consumption, I was horrified to see a big blob of cream cheese goo on her chest. I gasped involuntarily because for a second I thought maybe I'd hit a pothole and the ensuing bounce hurt my precious kid. Or perhaps she'd come down with a ferociously fast case of food poisoning. But then it dawned on me that the blob was in the shape of a perfect circle, almost as if it had been stamped with a cookie cutter. And I realized with growing frustration that my precious daughter had purposely twisted her bagel apart and smashed it on her navy-blue shirt in stubborn defiance!

So, I did what parents have been doing since Henry Ford invented automobiles in which we tote our precocious progeny around while they ignore us and text on their phones: I jerked the car over to the shoulder of the road, causing a dramatic spray of gravel, and bellowed, "I CAN'T BELIEVE YOU JUST DID THAT, YOUNG LADY! THAT WAS TOTALLY UNCALLED FOR! WE DO NOT PULL STUNTS LIKE THAT IN THIS FAMILY!" Then, as if my making-a-mountain-out-of-a-cream-cheese-molehill tirade wasn't enough, I finished the angry spiel with a word that's not in the Bible. Since this is a Christian book, that particular word will not appear in print, but it's not a term I'd use in front of my pastor. At least not on purpose! And the moment that ugly expletive flew out of my mouth, Missy gasped, and her eyes widened in shock. After staring at me in dismay for a few seconds, she announced accusingly, "Mom, Jesus does NOT like it when you say that word."

You'd think that would've been enough to put a plug in my piehole. But nope, I had an encore, which I bellowed even louder for emphasis: **"IF JESUS WAS HERE, HE WOULD'VE SAID IT TOO!"**

Yikes, nothing like a vocational Bible teacher spewing something about Jesus that's utterly indefensible according to Scripture! And what in the world does this confession have to do with theology, besides underscoring my glaring, perpetual need for divine grace? Well, basically everything, because theology is so much more about developing intimacy with our Creator Redeemer than it is about dumbfounding our church friends with multisyllabic seminary terms. And the closer we get to our Savior, the more we'll begin to resemble Him and bear the Fruit of the Spirit, and thus our mildly rebellious loved ones will be more apt to receive our patience than our wrath! Sound biblical theology won't necessarily make us smarter, but it should definitely make us more Christlike.

Taking the Plunge

All too often, biblically orthodox theology (that is, a belief system and worldview that are based on the promises and parameters found in the Holy Scriptures) is perceived as a lofty, somewhat sterile subject pursued by academics and seminarians. But if theology was merely a scholastic system through which people could organize their thoughts and suppositions about God and it didn't lead to the love of Jesus Christ, it would be the religious version of entomology—we might as well be pinning dead bugs to a corkboard. Theology was meant to be *lived*, and our Creator Redeemer is not a proposition to be examined; He's a personhood whom we get to engage with and ultimately emulate!

> Theology was meant to be *lived*.

For those of you who identify as type A, Enneagram one, or Enneagram eight, or who simply want to temporarily mute that chick in your small group who tends to commandeer conversations by parroting what she's heard on podcasts or YouTube, the "official" definition for theology is as follows:

> **theology** (Gk. θεολογία), lit. the "science of God." Among the Greek Fathers it comes to have two specific references: it can denote either the doctrine of the Trinity (i.e., of God's being, as opposed to his dealings with the created order), or it can mean prayer (as it is only in prayer that God is truly known). Later it came to mean the science of the Divinely revealed religious truths. Its theme is the Being and Nature of God and His creatures and the whole complex of the Divine dispensation from the Fall of Adam to the

Redemption through Christ and its mediation to men by His Church, including the so-called natural truths of God, the soul, the moral law, etc., which are accessible to mere reason. Its purpose is the investigation of the contents of belief by means of reason enlightened by faith (*fides quaerens intellectum*) and the promotion of its deeper understanding. In the course of time theology has developed into several branches, among them dogmatic, historical, and practical theology. The methods of classification of the sub-disciplines, however, fluctuate in different theological systems.[1]

Now don't worry, we're about to responsibly truncate that complicated mouthful of a definition! The original Greek root words that the English word *theology* is translated from are *theos*, which refers to God, and *logos* or *logia*, which refer to utterances, sayings, or words. Therefore, the basic definition of *theology* is "conversations about God." And conversation implies relationship, right? Furthermore, genuine relationships framed in the context of conversation are not purely transactional; they're personal. They require some measure of mental energy and emotional engagement. They affect our minds and our hearts. The tempo and trajectory of our day can be changed by one conversation, can't it?

Prior to his death in 2021, Dr. Bruce Demarest, who was a beloved professor at Denver Seminary (where I studied

> The basic definition of *theology* is "conversations about God."

---

[1]. *The Oxford Dictionary of the Christian Church*, 3rd ed., eds. F. L. Cross and Elizabeth A. Livingstone (New York: Oxford University Press, 2005), s.v. "theology."

for a doctorate, thereby proving old dogs really can learn new tricks!), was a renowned biblical scholar for decades *before* he learned to lean into God's embrace. He explains the spiritual journey from brilliant academic to beloved son in poignant detail in his book *Satisfy Your Soul: Restoring the Heart of Christian Spirituality*:

> Strangely enough, while conservative Christians have distrusted human intellect, we have relied heavily on the teaching of Bible doctrine to produce mature Christians. It hasn't worked, and now we're getting the picture: The soul begins to die when we view the faith chiefly as a set of intellectual propositions. Just as the thought of food will not satisfy an empty stomach, cognitive truth alone is not sufficient to form and nourish the Christian soul. What the inner man longs for is knowledge of God that comes from encountering, grappling with, participating with God in all levels of human experience—mind, body, and spirit. We were made to crave God with our whole being.[2]

Dr. Demarest's story resonates deeply with me, not because I'm a brilliant scholar but because for far too long I was more comfortable working hard on God's behalf than reclining against His breast. Dating back to the first Bible study I led in high school and well into adulthood, much of my desire to accrue knowledge about God and His Word was fueled by feelings of inadequacy. I was so afraid someone would look under the hood of my life and find me to

---

2. Dr. Bruce Demarest, *Satisfy Your Soul: Restoring the Heart of Christian Spirituality* (Colorado Springs: NavPress, 1999), 29.

be a fraud. It took an emotional crisis in my forties—which I later came to realize was designed by our compassionate Redeemer to eviscerate the shame and self-reliance that were slowly choking the hope and peace out of me—to finally learn that information *about* God is a poor substitute for intimacy *with* Him.

Theology is so much more than a system to organize our thoughts about God and so much better than a belief system to modify our behavior and ensure we won't say bad words when our children smear cream cheese goo on their Christian school uniforms—instead, it's a gorgeous, curving, adventure-strewn path that leads us deeper and deeper into the unconditional love of the one true God. Sound biblical theology doesn't produce smug scholars; it produces grateful and passionately devoted—albeit still flawed—disciples of Jesus Christ.

If you've put your hope in Jesus Christ and have begun to get to know Him better through Scripture, then the Holy Spirit will guide you and affirm that God's Word is inerrant for His intended kingdom purposes, but He never intended this sacred text to be used as a club to beat up on His image bearers! The Bible isn't a rule book or a collection of morality tales; at its core it is a divine love story, and the parameters we find in this redemptive narrative were written for our *good*—they're promissory and protective for God's people, not punitive. Every single word God breathed needs to be understood and applied under the canopy of His grace. And as we begin our descent into the wonderful waters of biblically orthodox theology, let's keep in mind that the Bible itself is not the treasure we're seeking; *Jesus is.*

Finding Treasure in Divine Depths

Soon after I met my now bestie, Australian Christine Caine, about fifteen years ago, she confided boldly, "Lisa, I've noticed how American Christian culture tends to try and wedge the Holy Scriptures right up there alongside God the Father, God the Son, and God the Spirit. But you know, the Bible is not actually a member of the Trinity." I was initially speechless (which in my case is a rarity along the lines of Halley's Comet) and soon felt mildly traumatized. Goodness gracious, was she trying to minimize the authority of Scripture? Despite my genuine affection for Chris, I was tempted not to stand too close to her lest she be zapped by a divine lightning bolt! It wasn't until I began to peruse N. T. Wright's literary masterpieces about the supremacy of Jesus/Logos to the inscripturated text/logos that my anxious heart stopped wringing its hands:

> All authority is from God, declares Paul in relation to governments (Rom. 13:1); Jesus says something very similar in John 19:11. In Matthew 28:18, the risen Jesus makes the still more striking claim that all authority in heaven and on earth has been given to him, a statement echoed elsewhere—for instance, in Philippians 2:9–11. A quick glance through many other texts in both the Old Testament (e.g., Isa. 40–55) and the New (e.g., Rev. 4 and 5) would confirm this kind of picture. When John declares that "in the beginning was the word," he does not reach a climax with "and the word was written down" but "and the word became flesh." The letter to the Hebrews speaks glowingly of God speaking through scripture in time past, but insists that now, at last, God has spoken through his own son

(1:1–2). Since these are themselves "scriptural" statements, that means that scripture itself points—authoritatively, if it does indeed possess authority!—away from itself and to the fact that final and true authority belongs to God himself, now delegated to Jesus Christ.[3]

I was dumbfounded in a doctoral class a few years ago—which wasn't at all uncommon!—but this particular time it had to do with the relationship between Jesus, who's called *the Word* in John 1, and *the word of God* in Hebrews 4:12, which I've always been taught referred to the Bible. I used to proudly quote it—"For the word of God is alive and active. Sharper than any double-edged sword, it penetrates even to dividing soul and spirit, joints and marrow; it judges the thoughts and attitudes of the heart"—while swinging my Bible around to make the point more dramatically when speaking at conferences and events. Based on my early experience in the extremely demonstrative church my dad attended after he and Mom divorced, I assumed gesticulating passionately *with* a Bible while teaching and quoting *from* the Bible was required behavior for anyone who wanted to be an effective communicator of the gospel. Which I instantly regretted one evening early in my vocation as a Bible teacher when I was the guest speaker at a Women in the Word event held in a lovely little Baptist church. I had gotten all worked up about a passage, and when I swung the personally engraved NIV Bible that my mom gave me for Christmas my senior year in high school, the entire book of Genesis ripped free from the binding, shot over the altar,

---

3. N. T. Wright, *Scripture and the Authority of God: How to Read the Bible Today* (Nashville: HarperCollins, 2005), 21–22.

and struck an elderly woman, who was piously sitting in the front pew, smack in the chest. It's a wonder she didn't sue my silly, Bible-hurling self.

I trust none of you have succumbed to any unnecessary Bible hurling, but my guess is that a few of us could still use some realignment when it comes to handling God's inscripturated Word, so I'll start us off with a couple of easy questions:

- *"The Word of God is sharper than a _____."*

  If you said, "two-edged sword," you hit it right on the chest, ahem, I mean nose!
- *That verse is found in _____ [book, chapter, and verse].*

  If you said, "Hebrews 4:12," you are two for two!
- *What's the overarching theme of the book of Hebrews?*

  If you said, "the superiority of Jesus Christ to the Old Covenant and the sole sufficiency of His atonement for our salvation," you are cooking with gas, baby!
- *Who was the original audience that Hebrews was preached to before it was inscribed as an epistle?*

  If you said, "first-century Jewish believers who were seriously considering apostasy because of the widespread oppression, abuse, and martyrdom they were experiencing in their polytheistic, largely pagan culture that was led by megalomaniac emperors who were paranoid about the possibility that Christianity could usurp their absolute power and

control," you have hereby earned a pass from volunteering in the church nursery for at least a month!
- *When was Hebrews written?*

  If you said, "between AD 60 and 70, and it couldn't have been later than AD 70 because that's when the temple was destroyed, which is featured prominently in the text," your name will be shouted from small group rooftops!
- *And does anyone have a clue when the Bible as we know it—with both Old and New Testaments—was canonized?*

  If you said, "The first unofficial canon of New Testament Scripture was compiled by Marcion of Sinope around AD 140, but the first comprehensive and official canon of the Christian Bible didn't exist until Athanasius compiled it in the fourth century, and it wasn't formally canonized until the councils of Hippo and Carthage in AD 393 and AD 419," I will personally come to your house and scrub your floors!

Here's the point I'm trying to make—the author of Hebrews wasn't talking about a leather-bound Christian Bible when he preached that the Word of God was living and active and sharper than a two-edged sword because it didn't even exist back then! However, the original Greek word—*logos*—that's translated "word of God" in Hebrews 4 is the exact same word used to describe Jesus in John 1, so in light of the historical context of Hebrews, chapter 4, verse 12 must be referring to the resurrected Messiah! Jesus is *alive and active.* He is *sharper than any double-edged sword, able to penetrate even to dividing soul and spirit, joints and marrow!* He is the One able to *judge the thoughts and attitudes of our hearts.* And the fact that Jesus is the main subject here in Hebrews becomes even more evident in the following verse: "No creature is hidden from *him*, but all things are naked and exposed to the eyes of *him* to whom we must give an account" (v. 13 CSB, emphasis mine).

Surely one of the saddest, most sobering observations our incarnate Messiah made about spiritual leaders (in this case, Jewish leaders) is found in John 5:

> I have testimony weightier than that of John. For the works that the Father has given me to finish—the very works that I am doing—testify that the Father has sent me. And the Father who sent me has himself testified concerning me. You have never heard his voice nor seen his form, nor does his word dwell in you, for you do not believe the one he sent. *You study the Scriptures diligently because you think that in them you have eternal life. These are the very Scriptures that testify about me, yet you refuse to come to me to have life.* (vv. 36–40, emphasis mine)

In other words, *You've mastered the Old Testament, but you missed ME.* Which leads me to why the title of this book is *A Jesus-Shaped Life.* If our pursuit of biblically orthodox theology doesn't ultimately have a Christoformic effect on us—which is just a fancy way of saying we're being consistently transformed into a more Christlike way of living—thereby drawing others toward Jesus Himself, then our pursuit is at best shallow, at worst sabotaged by self-serving

Helpful Hooks to Hang Theological Content On

Epignosis: the Greek word for knowledge with understanding, relating to knowledge of transcendent value. In the New Testament, *epignōsis* generally refers to knowledge of a spiritual or moral nature such as awareness of one's sinfulness (Rom. 3:20) or knowledge of God (Col. 1:10) or his truth (Titus 1:1). The word is used 20 times in the NT. The three times the word is used in the letter to the Romans, it refers to spiritual blindness, not having the true knowledge that points to God. In every occurrence outside of Romans (that is, the remaining 17 times), *epignōsis* indicates spiritual understanding such as knowledge of the truth (1 Tim. 2:4; 2 Tim. 2:25; Titus 1:1; Heb. 10:26), knowledge of God (Eph. 1:17; Col. 3:10; 2 Pet. 1:2–8), or knowledge of God's will (Phil. 1:9; Col. 1:9). Therefore, epignosis can loosely be translated as *heart knowledge*.

Gnosis: the Greek word for knowledge. The term "gnosticism" (derived from *gnōsis*) was first used in the 18th century to refer to a current in the religious life of late antiquity which had direct bearing on the development of the belief and practice of the early church. The term has traditionally functioned in a pejorative sense because *gnostics* understood themselves to be the elite "chosen people" who, in distinction from the "worldly-minded," were able to perceive the delicate connection between world (cosmology), humanity (anthropology), and salvation (soteriology). The goal of gnostic teaching was that with the help of insight (*gnōsis*), the elect could be freed from the fetters of this world (spirit

> from matter, light from darkness) and so return to their true home in the Kingdom of Light—for that alone is the meaning of "salvation." It is not a matter of deliverance from sin and guilt, as in orthodoxy, but of the freeing of the spirit from matter (*hyle*), in particular, the material human body. In the course of time, gnostics developed a coherent conceptual framework from both their myths and their practice in behavior and cultus. Their mythology consisted of an "exegetical protest" against the older and widely accepted biblical and ecclesiastical traditions. Therefore, gnosis can be loosely translated as *head knowledge*.
>
> Jeremiah K. Garrett, "Knowledge," in *Lexham Theological Wordbook*, Lexham Bible Reference Series, ed. Douglas Mangum et al. (Bellingham, WA: Lexham Press, 2014); Kurt Rudolph, "Gnosticism," in *The Anchor Yale Bible Dictionary*, ed. David Noel Freedman (New York: Doubleday, 1992), 1033–34

motives. Biblical *orthodoxy* (what we believe to be true of God) must lead to Christoformic *orthopraxy* (how we live in light of what we believe to be true of God).

As we dive deeper into biblically orthodox theology, it's likely that most of us will have to jettison theology we've inherited along the way and sincerely thought was true. And sometimes it's tough to let go of thoughts and patterns we believed were biblically based and God-honoring, so it behooves us to take a deep breath and maybe even guzzle a caffeinated beverage drizzled with chocolate sauce and topped with whipped cream before reading the next statement:

> **More often than not, the phrase "word of God" in the New Testament isn't used to describe a physical Bible; instead, it's referring to Jesus.**

(Okay, now please take another deep breath and a long gulp of that dessert disguised as coffee before forging ahead.)

For instance, when Paul tells Timothy to "preach the word" (2 Tim. 4:2), he's not talking about expository teaching; he's encouraging young Tim to keep Jesus at the center of every message he shares! I think one of the reasons we have such a high rate of biblical illiteracy among believers today is that we've segregated Jesus—Logos—from our leather-bound copies of God's promises and parameters. But the good news is that when we stop framing the Word of God as merely truthful data to wrap our ethics around and begin to connect it to the work and person of JESUS CHRIST, we'll quit beating people up with it, and we will become increasingly convinced that He loves us *and* them!

Leaning into the Shape of Living Water

Speaking of all things Christocentric and the necessary synergy between our orthodoxy and orthopraxy, there's a long list of ancient, Jesus-shaped theologians I greatly admire and esteem, like Saint Augustine, Thomas à Kempis, and Madame Jeanne Guyon, but one of the more modern saints I've grown to appreciate these past few years is Ray S. Anderson. And I owe him a fancy dinner when we meet in Glory (he passed away in 2009) because that dear saint unwittingly lifted the weight of not wearing a WWJD bracelet off my heavily burdened shoulders through this excerpt from his book *The Shape of Practical Theology*:

> The same Jesus who inspired the true account of his own life and ministry through the Holy Spirit in the form of

Scripture continues to be present in the act of reading, hearing and interpreting the Scriptures. Thus, Scripture is not merely a product that was "made" by the inspiration of the Holy Spirit and from which the maker can be detached, but Scripture continues to be the particular form of Christopraxis that provides a normative and objective basis for the life of the church. But because Scripture is a form of Christopraxis, its infallibility is located in the Christ of Scripture as the only true Word of God and not merely in Scripture as a product of inspiration that could somehow be detached from Christ.

In this way, it can be said that Jesus is not only the subject of proclamation (the one about whom we preach), but he is himself the proclaimer in every act of proclamation (the one who proclaims himself through the event of preaching). *Theological reflection does not ask the question "What would Jesus do in this situation?" because this question would imply his absence. Rather, it asks the question "Where is Jesus in this situation and what am I to do as a minister?"* When the Scripture is interpreted in such a way that direction is sought for lives who need to be conformed to the true and healing power of God's Word, we must remember that Jesus is not only the "author" of Scripture through the power of the Spirit, but he himself is a "reader" and interpreter of Scripture in every contemporary moment.[4]

Wowzers, did you get that? "Theological reflection does not ask the question 'What would Jesus do in this situation?' because this question would imply his absence. Rather, it

---

4. Ray S. Anderson, *The Shape of Practical Theology: Empowering Ministry with Theological Praxis* (Downer's Grove, IL: InterVarsity Press, 2001), 55–56, emphasis mine.

asks the question 'Where is Jesus in this situation and what am I to do as a minister?'" That put an arrow right through the heart of my residual WWJD guilt and helped me exhale into the embrace of Jesus!

When I brought Missy home from Haiti, following our two-year adoption journey (I've often described our experience as hiking up a mountain on Rollerblades—in a downpour!), my counselor said what Missy needed was safety and security. She explained that the most effective way for me to communicate love to her was through consistency, patience, and gentle physical touch. Then she reasoned that while Missy displayed a healthy level of dependence on me because of my regular visits to spend time with her in Haiti during our adoption process, her overall wariness would likely linger for a while since her first four years of life were riddled with abandonment and abuse. Her little heart needed time to trust that I wouldn't leave her too.

The first night we got home we were both so exhausted after getting up in the middle of the previous night and trekking from the orphanage to the Port-au-Prince airport, then on to the Miami airport, then through customs, then through an intense international adoption interrogation mandated by the Department of Homeland Security, then back through security in Miami, and on to the Nashville airport, then walking down the C concourse to a raucous group of one-hundred-plus dear friends who were waiting for us outside of baggage claim, and finally arriving home to our little farmette south of Nashville, that I don't remember much about that first bedtime. However, the second night I was getting Missy settled into her bed, I began rubbing her rough little feet with shea butter (she went barefoot a lot in Haiti, and her precious feet were covered with cracks and callouses) while she watched me solemnly with her big brown eyes. Then I lay down beside her and said, "Missy, ou trè bel. Ou trè brav. Ou trè entèlijan," which is Creole—her native language—for *Missy, you're very beautiful. You're very brave. You're very intelligent.* Then I said, "Missy, man-man renmen w anpil anpil men jezi renmen ou plis," which is Creole for *Mama loves you very, very much, but Jesus loves you even more.*

Night after night I repeated those phrases after rubbing my baby girl's feet with shea butter. For the first two weeks, Missy couldn't look at me while I spoke. She'd literally turn her head in the opposite direction and sometimes almost imperceptibly shake her head back and forth, as if respectfully disagreeing with the affirmations I was speaking over her. Which made sense because I'm sure no one at the orphanage told her she was beautiful or brave or intelligent. In fact, one of the nannies there confided in me that Missy would never be able to read or write, and I should just be grateful she had the mental capacity to sing. I was stunned that this insensitive woman couldn't see the miracle right in front of her eyes—how an innocent toddler who'd lost her birth mom and was sick with tuberculosis and barely able to breathe for years, who also suffered from severe malnutrition and had a growling stomach for most of her young life, who was finally sent to a "safe" orphanage where she had to endure regular beatings by supposed caretakers because they deeply resented having to touch an HIV-positive baby girl, *still* had enough tenacious hope to *sing* in such deplorable conditions. My beautiful, brave, intelligent daughter defied odds that many adults would deem insurmountable.

By the third week, Missy began to glance in my direction when I was telling her how beautiful and brave and smart she was but would quickly turn away before I got to the part where I told her how much I loved her and how Jesus loved her even more. After an entire month of the exact same affectionate and affirming bedtime ritual, Missy finally held my gaze throughout the massage and recitation. When I finished with the usual benediction of *I love you very, very much, but Jesus loves you even more*, she questioned me softly: "Mama love Missy?" My heart leapt over the sweet wonder in her tone, and my eyes filled with tears. Everything in me wanted to scoop her up and hug her fiercely, but something in me knew that she needed a response, so without breaking eye contact, I replied, "Oh, honey, I love you more than I know how to explain. I didn't even know that I *could* love someone this much until I became your second mama. In fact, I think I've broken a few ribs because my heart is so crammed full of love for you that it had to expand in my chest!" She giggled shyly over my ardent response and rotated her entire body toward me until we were facing each other in that tiny twin bed. Then with a twinkle in her eyes, she proclaimed with matching enthusiasm, "Mama *love* Missy!" Her question became a declaration.

A few seconds later, that miracle child of mine inched her perfect brown toes up my belly until she found a crease I christened "the valley of affection." I grew it out of profound love for this daughter I don't deserve—and because I assumed the calories in all those Chick-fil-A waffle fries I'd been wolfing down since bringing her home wouldn't count since it's a Christian-owned company! She purposely poked all ten toes into my tummy crack and let out a heavy sigh, at which point she let her weight collapse into the soft warmth of the mattress. Then her eyelids started to flutter, and right before giving way to slumber, she murmured contently, "Mama *love* Missy."

The quest for deeper, truer, efficacious, and biblically orthodox theology requires sharp, inquisitive minds. But it also requires tender hearts that have remained pliant with tenacious hope. If you and I can learn to lean so closely into the intimate and unconditional love of Jesus that we can purposely stick our proverbial toes into the crevasse of His kindness on this quest, it'll have the power to slowly but surely mold our lives into a shape somewhat like His, and quite possibly, that can help transform our tiny corner of this great big, beautiful world we call home for now.

TWO

Our God Is a Perfect "Us"

> The doctrine of the Trinity is not extraneous or supplementary or an obscure appendage to the Christian faith. It is the heart of the Gospel.
>
> Saint Augustine

Recently, Missy, my dear friend Allison, and I got to go on a humanitarian trip with a Convoy of Hope team to the Dominican Republic. The podcast Alli and I record together (*Back Porch Theology*) is partnering with Convoy to help single moms get sustainable jobs so that their children can be rescued from the poverty, the food scarcity, and all too often the sexual abuse they've had to endure. It was an undeserved privilege to get to spend time with all those brave moms, but there's one in particular I'll never forget. Her name is Maria. We met at a landfill (which is polite vernacular for "dump") on the outskirts of a large, metropolitan city with the same kind of malls you'd see in

America. People started dumping their trash at this landfill thirty-plus years ago, and unlike in the US, there's no system for burning, compacting, or recycling the refuse. Therefore, like a putrid onion, layer upon layer of garbage has been accumulating for so long that the "mountains" you see far off in the distance are actually giant piles of rubbish. Currently almost fifteen thousand people—most of them undocumented Haitians—call this landfill home and spend their time rummaging through the filthy, discarded junk for items to resell or scraps of food to feed their family.

Maria and I conversed through a translator while our children played together. She was curious as to why my daughter was Black. When I explained how Missy's first mom had died in a rural Haitian village, after which I began the adoption process, her eyes widened. Haitians—especially those who are undocumented, impoverished, and live at the dump—are barely tolerated by most Dominicans; therefore, she was surprised that I (who she presumed to be a wealthy American) would "choose" a Haitian daughter. When I explained that our little family was a divinely authored miracle because Missy wasn't expected to live when we first started the adoption journey and how I was way too old to get pregnant—besides the fact that I was single like her!—her eyes filled with tears. Then when I told her that getting to be Missy's second mama was the second greatest gift in my whole life—second only to my relationship with Jesus—she reached out and took hold of both of my hands.

With a shaky voice she thanked me for loving Haitians. Then she squeezed my hands tighter, leaned so close that I could see the dark pupils in her beautiful brown eyes, and begged me to please, PLEASE take one of her eight children back to Tennessee with us so that at least one of her precious sons or daughters could have the same shot at a healthy, hope-filled life that Missy did.

Of course, I did my best to assure her that despite their difficult circumstances, God had chosen her to parent her kids and with His help they would be blessed. I reminded her that tangible relief was right around the corner because once the tilapia (fish) farm we were building was up and running, they'd have enough food to eat and they'd have product to sell, which meant she'd soon be able to afford the documentation process that would allow her children to enroll in school. But the only thing I did that seemed a tiny bit helpful to Maria in that moment was to hold her close for several long minutes until her frail shoulders stopped shaking with sobs.

When you peel back just a layer or two of culture, tradition, and socioeconomic variables, it's incredible how much we humans have in common. How we all yearn for genuine connection. How most of us would do almost anything to protect our families. How even a small kindness among us has the power to transcend a myriad of barriers and form the rebar of real relationship.

Which brings us to the subject of the Trinity, the fact that God is perfectly triune in nature—monotheistic yet consisting of three equally divine and fully distinguished "persons"—always existing as God the Father, God the Son, and God the Holy Spirit. While this is a profound doctrinal concept that most theologians (at least the ones I respect!) would profess to be the primary wall of Christian orthodoxy, at its core the Trinity proves that our Creator Redeemer is a relational God. He exists in a perfect community unto

Himself, and He invites us into that community of unconditional love via a relationship with Jesus Christ. Yes, it's hard to wrap our finite human minds around the complexities of the Trinity, but if you've ever experienced loneliness, you'll find your heart gravitating to its intrinsic promise of belonging. Not only does our God exist in triune community, He sent His only begotten Son to envelop us into His forever family, and He compassionately seals His relational commitment to us with His Spirit, whose role is to remind us over and over again that we have the right to call the Ruler of the Universe "Dad" (Rom. 8:15). Sure, there may be moments in time when we *feel* alone, but the profound takeaway of the trinitarian nature of God means that we never actually are.

Taking the Plunge

Remember when those perky parenting influencers on social media began advocating hiding vegetables in kids' food to ensure they'd get the nutrients they need? Well, I tried to sneak some veggies into Missy's meals a few years ago, and it did not go over nearly as well as those perfectly coiffed moms of Instagram implied it would. All it took was one look at the green flecks of spinach in her pancakes to cause her smile to turn down into a frown, after which she proclaimed she wasn't hungry. Same for the cauliflower masquerading as mashed potatoes. No amount of butter can camouflage that hot mess. I've learned to be straightforward with my kid about how her body needs the nutrients in fresh vegetables in order to be strong and healthy to get her to eat them. Well, that and I threatened to take away some of her allotted iPad time! Fortunately, now she likes the taste of vegetables, except for cauliflower—that's still a no-go—and broccoli, which she insists tastes like little trees! Here's the deal, y'all—the next few paragraphs are *good for you*. Because wrapping your mind around the historical background of the Trinity will help you wrap your heart more tightly around God. And some of this stuff will eventually start tasting as good to your spirit as hot Chick-fil-A waffle fries, I promise.

Early in Constantine's reign as the emperor of Rome (he reigned from AD 306 to 337) he had a dream the night before facing his brother-in-law Maxentius at the Battle of the Milvian Bridge. There are two differing accounts of Constantine's dramatic experience: one authored by Eusebius, who was one of his court bishops, and one authored by Lucius, who was one of his court advisers. Eusebius insisted the emperor envisioned the cross of Jesus Christ, while Lucius insisted that he had a dream about the Greek letters *chi* and *rho*, which are the first two letters in the title "Christ." But regardless of the specific details of his dream/vision, historical records are unanimous that he won the military clash the following day, credited his victory to God's intervention, and converted to Christianity as a result. In so doing, he changed the course of history.

Prior to Constantine's public acknowledgment of faith in Jesus Christ, Christians were a very small minority of the world's population and were severely persecuted throughout the ancient world. Although the Roman Empire was a pluralistic society that tolerated many religious beliefs and considered them *licita* (the Latin word for "recognized"), Christianity was not officially recognized nor protected by the Roman Empire. And since Christ followers pledged their allegiance to one Triune God instead of worshiping some—better yet, all—of the 265 little "g" gods that the Roman Empire formally allowed, many of their fellow citizens branded Christianity a suspicious cult and a danger to national unity.

Furthermore, Christians refused to participate in emperor worship, which was widely practiced and even required by most Roman rulers during that era. It went down like this: A couple of times a year, Roman citizens, and anyone else under Roman rule, had to burn incense at an altar and declare their allegiance to whichever emperor happened to be in charge at the time. Which may not sound like a big deal to you initially, but there were a few dictators who were deadly serious about the whole emperor worship thing.

Emperor Caligula (who ruled from AD 37 to 41) forced soldiers to take images of him into the Jewish temple, and when the Jews revolted, he drafted a decree to have them all murdered. Thankfully, he was overthrown before his homicidal decree could be carried out! Emperor Domitian (who ruled from AD 81 to 96) had people executed if they refused to call him "Lord." Another well-known Roman emperor, Nero, not only was incensed that Christians wouldn't bow their knee to his authority in worship, but he also misunderstood the concept of communion and assumed that Christians were practicing cannibalism when they talked about drinking "Christ's blood" and eating "His body" in remembrance of the crucifixion and resurrection. Which is why our great-great-great-and-then-some grandmothers and grandfathers of the faith were the perfect scapegoats to blame when one of his devious plans went awry.

Historians paint Emperor Nero as the master arsonist behind the Great Fire of Rome in AD 64 because he was waning in popularity, so he schemed up a nefarious plan in which his minions would secretly set the city on fire while he was away on "business," then he'd ride back into town in a blaze of glory (pun intended), extinguish the flames with his army, stage a massive remodeling campaign, and eventually come out smelling like the heroic rose who saved Rome and developed her to even greater glory, thus ensuring his ongoing political juggernaut. But by the time those notorious flames began to spread, rumors of his treachery were already circulating, which were the genesis of the infamous phrase, "Nero fiddled while Rome burned!"

Of course, when Nero realized his plan had backfired (pun intended here too), he knew he needed someone else to blame, so he pointed to that small motley crew of first-century Christians—who most people already thought were weird—and said, "Those crazy cannibals—they're the ones who started the fire!" Adding horrific insult to cruel injury, over the years he had his soldiers arrest thousands of believers on trumped-up charges, and then he had them impaled on stakes, covered with tar, and set on fire around the perimeter of his palace for "entertainment."

When you consider the persecution, prejudice, subjugation, and suffering that Christians had to endure for the first three hundred years following the earthly ministry of Jesus Christ, Constantine's salvation is kind of like Darth

Vader turning his back on the evil empire and becoming a Jedi! Mind you, his reign wasn't altogether righteous—some historians believe he had both his wife and son executed, along with some Egyptian priests who didn't live up to his moral standards—but God used that mistake-prone man to establish the scaffolding that our Christian belief system is built on.

Not long after he trusted in Jesus Christ, Constantine realized there were some cray-cray teachers in the family of faith whose errant sermons about Jesus being of a lesser nature than God were threatening to burn down our then-fledgling theological framework just as surely as Nero's pet fire eviscerated Rome. In order to counteract those heretical yahoos who had infiltrated Christian circles and were talking smack about Jesus, which was causing confusion among believers, Constantine ordered all the bishops to meet together in the city of Nicaea for the first formal Christian council in AD 325. Their assignment was to prayerfully consider two questions: *How does this teaching stack up against the whole of what Scripture teaches?* and *What are the implications of this teaching regarding our salvation through Jesus?*

Ultimately, the Council of Nicaea (there were seven ecumenical councils in total from AD 325 to 787, all of which were convened to establish a consensus of Christian orthodoxy) established the essential doctrine of the Trinity, which is clearly expressed in the spiritual "manifesto" that came out of that inaugural ecumenical convention, the Nicene Creed (now more accurately known as the Niceno-Constantinopolitan Creed because it was revised at the Council of Constantinople in 381):

We believe in one God,
the Father, the Almighty
maker of heaven and earth,
of all that is, seen and unseen.

We believe in one Lord, Jesus Christ,
the only Son of God,
eternally begotten of the Father,
God from God, Light from Light,
true God from true God,
begotten, not made,
of one Being with the Father.
Through him all things were made.
For us and for our salvation
he came down from heaven:
by the power of the Holy Spirit
he became incarnate from the Virgin Mary,
and was made man.
For our sake he was crucified under Pontius Pilate;
he suffered death and was buried.
On the third day he rose again
in accordance with the Scriptures;
he ascended into heaven
and is seated at the right hand of the Father.
He will come again in glory to judge the living and
    the dead,
and his kingdom will have no end.

We believe in the Holy Spirit, the Lord, the giver of
    life,
who proceeds from the Father and the Son.
With the Father and the Son he is worshiped and
    glorified.
He has spoken through the Prophets.

> We believe in one holy catholic and apostolic Church.
> We acknowledge one baptism for the forgiveness of sins.
> We look for the resurrection of the dead, and the life of the world to come. Amen.[1]

Mind you, the concept of the Trinity had already been percolating in the minds of early church fathers. More than a hundred years before that first Council of Nicaea a godly brainiac named Tertullian (AD 160–220) affirmed that the Godhead consisted of one substance/*substantia* with three distinct persons/*personae*, resulting in a "unity in Trinity."[2] And since theology (aka conversations about God!) is never stagnant, things kept moving along the anthropological trinitarian freeway, because a little more than two hundred years after the Nicene/Niceno-Constantinopolitan Creed was adopted as a declarative standard of Christian faith, a small but significant and very controversial addition called the filioque clause was made at the anti-Arian Council of Toledo in 589.[3] (This addition to the creed ultimately led to the schism between the Roman Catholic Church and the Eastern Orthodox Tradition—and it's pronounced *fee-lee-oh-quay*.) *Filioque* is a fancy Latin term that means "and from the Son." And it was included in the Nicene/Niceno-Constantinopolitan

---

1. The Nicene Creed, Anglican Compass, https://anglicancompass.com/the-niceno-constantinopolitan-creed/.
2. Tertullian, Prax. 2.
3. Charles Meeks, "Trinity," in *The Lexham Bible Dictionary*, eds. John D. Barry, David Bomar, Derek R. Brown, Rachel Klippenstein, Douglas Mangum, Carrie Sinclair Wolcott, Lazarus Wentz, Elliot Ritzema, and Wendy Widder (Bellingham, WA: Lexham Press, 2016).

What Exactly Is a Creed?

A creed is a formal pledge of allegiance to a set of doctrinal statements concerning God and His relationship to His creation. The English word "creed" comes from the Latin *credo*, meaning "I believe." It expresses personal trust in a body of beliefs. Creeds are typically characterized by the following features:

- an authoritative summary statement of belief affirmed by a believer or a community of believers
- stable, fixed wording
- composition or authorization by a synod or magisterium, the sanction of ecclesiastical authority
- a summary of the essential articles of the particular religion or church for which it serves as a test of orthodoxy

The term "creed" is more common in Protestant theology than in Roman Catholic and Orthodox theology, which usually speak of *symbola* or *dogmata* instead.

Arianism was a movement within the early church that distinguished the divinity of God the Father from the divinity of Christ by arguing that Jesus was a created being. The movement derived from the teachings of a leader named Arius who taught that Christ was a created being—the first one created by God the Father. This view made Christ subordinate to the Father and set off what is often called the "Arian controversy." Church leaders opposed Arianism because they felt it denied full divinity to Jesus. The debate over Arianism raged throughout the fourth century, but the

> now-orthodox view that Christ was co-equal and co-eternal with the Father was strongly defended by the Cappadocian fathers: Basil of Caesarea, Gregory of Nazianus, and Gregory of Nyssa. The orthodox view was ultimately accepted as the official position of the Church at the Council of Constantinople in 381. After this, Arianism gradually died out.
>
> Frank M. Hasel, "Creeds and Confessions," in Barry et al., *Lexham Bible Dictionary*; "Arianism," in *Lexham Bible Dictionary*

Creed to affirm that the Holy Spirit proceeds from the Father *and* the Son (the original version of the Nicene/Niceno-Constantinopolitan Creed stated that the Holy Spirit came from the Father, thereby unwittingly diminishing the authority of Jesus) to underscore the trinitarian nature and unity of our Creator Redeemer.

Not long afterward, in the eighth century, another oh-so-wise church father, John of Damascus, began using the Greek term *perichoresis*, which means "a circle of perpetual movement" (it's also the term we derive the English word *choreography* from, so everyone who likes to dance, from Gene Kelly to Taylor Swift, should pay dear old John's descendants a royalty!), to describe the Trinity. In his brilliant work, *De Fide Orthodoxa*, he explains that the three Persons of the Trinity "are made one not so as to commingle, but so as to cleave to each other, and they have their being in each other without any coalescence or commingling."[4]

Thankfully, modern scholar Dr. Kevin DeYoung breaks perichoresis down into more bite-sized pieces:

---

4. John of Damascus, *De Fide Orthodoxa* 1.8, PG 94.829A.

The Greek term used to describe the eternal mutual indwelling of the persons of the Trinity is *perichoresis* (in Latin, *circumincession*). The word *circulatio* is also sometimes used as a way of metaphorically describing the unceasing circulation of the divine essence, such that each person is in the other two, while the others are in each one. At the risk of putting things in physical terms, perichoresis means that "all three persons occupy the same divine space." In other words, we cannot see God without seeing all three persons at the same time.

The mutual indwelling of perichoresis means two things. First, the three persons of the Trinity are all fully in one another. And second, each person of the Trinity is in full possession of the divine essence. To be sure, the Father is not the Son, the Son is not the Spirit, and the Spirit is not the Father. Perichoresis does not deny any of this. What perichoresis maintains is that you cannot have one person of the Trinity without having the other two, and you cannot have any person of the Trinity without having the fullness of God. The inter-communion of the persons is reciprocal, and their operations are inseparable.[5]

If you're tempted to take a mental health break right about now because all this trinitarian talk is confusing, please keep reading because I promise there's light at the end of this doctrinal tunnel.

Unless you've been daydreaming while skimming the last few paragraphs, you've probably picked up on the fact that the concept of the Trinity is more complex than a Rubik's

---

5. Kevin DeYoung, "Theological Primer: Perichoresis," The Gospel Coalition, November 19, 2020, https://www.thegospelcoalition.org/blogs/kevin-deyoung/theological-primer-perichoresis/.

Cube and trinitarian language doesn't invite easy models or metaphors! As a matter of fact, using H_2O as an example to explain the Trinity—which I was taught when I was a kid in Sunday school and used for much of my adult life—is an unfortunate example of modalism, which is a false doctrinal view that there is one God who has sequentially revealed himself as Father, Son, and Holy Spirit, yet each divine name is merely a mode of the one God's activity as opposed to a distinct person.[6] Although ice, water, and steam being three separate forms of the same element (H_2O) may sound like a symbolic slam dunk, our perfect, perpetual, trinitarian God can't be illustrated by ice, water, and steam because ice can't simultaneously exist as water, water can't simultaneously exist as steam, etc.

Now, before you hurl this book across the room and give up on understanding the complexity of the Trinity, please hang in there because this is kind of like delivering a broad-shouldered baby—based on what several friends who gave birth to XL newborns have told me, the moment they got to hold their linebacker-to-be babies, their excruciatingly painful labor faded into an inconsequential memory! Or, as one of my theological heroes Dr. Michael Bird explains more appropriately,

> At the end of the day, if we are going to know God better, we have to learn about the Trinity. We have to delve into how the church has explained who God is in light of its Scriptures and through its controversies and creeds. Only when we know who God is can we properly pray to him,

---

6. Michael Bird, *Evangelical Theology: A Biblical and Systematic Introduction*, 2nd ed. (Grand Rapids: Zondervan, 2020), 110.

worship him, proclaim him, imitate him, and serve him! This isn't easy. It means trying to penetrate an impenetrable mystery, catching a glimpse of it, and being left in wonder. It will take patience and hard work. You might feel like it is over your head, so lift up your head in order to understand. Once the study is done, the implications and applications will hopefully flow like milk and honey in the promised land of theological labor. As Augustine said, "There is no subject where error is more dangerous, research more laborious, and discovery more fruitful than the oneness of the Trinity [unitas trinitatis] of the Father, the Son, and the Holy Spirit."[7]

Finding Treasure in Divine Depths

I recently heard a struggling saint on a podcast who admitted they were in the process of "deconstructing" their Christianity and argued that the word *Trinity* isn't in the Bible. And technically they're right. But sadly, their angry opposition has blinded them to the nonliteral yet startlingly unmistakable miracle of the Trinity, which is apparent throughout Scripture. For instance, there's a Holy Spirit shout-out at the very beginning of the Bible:

> In the beginning God created the heavens and the earth. Now the earth was formless and empty, darkness was over the surface of the deep, and *the Spirit of God was hovering* over the waters. (Gen. 1:1–2, emphasis mine)

7. Bird, *Evangelical Theology*, 108–9.

Later on in that first chapter of the Good Book there's a trinitarian wink when Moses explains how God made humanity in His image:

> Then God said, "Let *us* make mankind in *our* image, in *our* likeness, so that they may rule over the fish in the sea and the birds in the sky, over the livestock and all the wild animals, and over all the creatures that move along the ground."
>
> So God created mankind in his own image,
> in the image of God he created them;
> male and female he created them. (vv. 26–27, emphasis mine)

Admittedly, there are some passages where the Trinity is more implied than explicit, like the "fourth man" in the fiery furnace with Shadrach, Meshach, and Abednego, whom ancient theologian Justin Martyr insisted was a Christophany—a visible appearance of preincarnate Jesus. Remember when Daniel's friends got hurled into a commercial oven because they refused to renounce their belief in the one true God and adopt King Nebuchadnezzar's polytheistic nonsense? (Okay, I'm taking a tiny bit of liberty with the Hebrew, but this is pretty close to what happened in Daniel 3!) But then their captors noticed they were miraculously unharmed *and* hanging out with another dude who looked "like a son of the gods" in that unbearably hot death chamber (Dan. 3:25).

However, there are lots of passages in which the Trinity pretty much jumps off the page, such as the scene of Jesus's baptism in Mark's Gospel:

At that time Jesus came from Nazareth in Galilee and was baptized by John in the Jordan. *Just as Jesus was coming up out of the water, he saw heaven being torn open and the Spirit descending on him like a dove. And a voice came from heaven: "You are my Son, whom I love; with you I am well pleased."* (Mark 1:9–11, emphasis mine)

As well as in Paul's benediction to the believers in Corinth:

Finally, brothers and sisters, rejoice! Strive for full restoration, encourage one another, be of one mind, live in peace. And the God of love and peace will be with you.

Greet one another with a holy kiss. All God's people here send their greetings.

May the grace of the Lord Jesus Christ, and the love of God, and the fellowship of the Holy Spirit be with you all. (2 Cor. 13:11–14, emphasis mine)

Now, let's head over to Luke's Gospel and compare Mary's Magnificat (her melodic response to finding out God chose her to be the mother of the long-awaited Messiah) to dear geriatric Simeon's exuberant song when he finally meets baby Jesus, and this trinitarian thread in Scripture becomes even more noticeable in the fabric of redemption:

Mary

My soul glorifies the Lord
    and my spirit rejoices in God *my Savior*,
for he has been mindful
    of the humble state of his servant.
From now on all generations will call me blessed,
    for the Mighty One has done great things for me—

> holy is his name.
> His mercy extends to those who fear him,
> > from generation to generation.
> He has performed mighty deeds with his arm;
> > he has scattered those who are proud in their inmost thoughts.
> He has brought down rulers from their thrones
> > but has lifted up the humble.
> He has filled the hungry with good things
> > but has sent the rich away empty.
> He has helped his servant Israel,
> > remembering to be merciful
> to Abraham and his descendants forever,
> > just as he promised our ancestors. (Luke 1:46–55, emphasis mine)

Simeon

Now there was a man in Jerusalem called Simeon, who was righteous and devout. He was waiting for *the consolation of Israel*, and the Holy Spirit was on him. It had been revealed to him by the Holy Spirit that he would not die before he had seen the Lord's Messiah. Moved by the Spirit, he went into the temple courts. When the parents brought in the child Jesus to do for him what the custom of the Law required, Simeon took him in his arms and praised God, saying [singing]:

> "Sovereign Lord, as you have promised,
> > you may now dismiss your servant in peace.
> For my eyes have seen *your salvation*,
> > which you have prepared in the sight of all nations:
> a light for revelation to the Gentiles,
> > and the glory of your people Israel." (Luke 2:25–32, emphasis mine)

You can almost hear the harmonious hum of the Trinity here at the beginning of Luke because the word Mary uses for "savior" is *sōtēr* in Greek, which means "deliverer" or "rescuer" (it's also the root of *soteriology*, which refers to the doctrine of salvation through Jesus Christ!). Then Simeon sings a derivative of the same word in his lyric, "your *salvation*," because *salvation* comes from the Greek word *sōtērion*. In other words, both teenage Mary and octogenarian Simeon are warbling about how Jesus is the *Savior* the world's longing for. But it gets even better when you back up to the word *consolation* at the beginning of the passage about Simeon, because it comes from the Greek word *paraklēsis*, which means "comfort" and is a derivative of the word *paraklētos*, which means "comforter" and is the term John uses to describe the Holy Spirit. It's an epic mic-drop moment for Bible nerds everywhere!

The bottom line is the redemptive metanarrative of Holy Writ (which is a more formal term for *the Bible* or *the Holy Scriptures* or what my dad's country preacher called *the Good Book*) loses its cohesion without the glue of the Trinity. Modern scholar Kevin J. Vanhoozer says it well: "The integrity of the gospel is fatally compromised if either the Son or the Spirit is not fully God. If the Son were not God, he could neither reveal the Father nor atone for our sin. If the Spirit were not God, he could unite us neither to the Father and Son nor one another. The gospel, then, requires a triune God."[8] If you're truly a Bible believer, you're on Team Trinity, whether you know it yet or not!

---

8. Kevin J. Vanhoozer, *Drama of Doctrine: A Canonical Linguistic Approach to Christian Theology* (Louisville: Westminster John Knox, 2005), 43.

Leaning into the Shape of Living Water

The first year we gathered in Franklin, Tennessee, for the Kerygma Summit in 2022, we were pleasantly surprised that female ministry leaders came from so many streams of the church—from pew-jumping Pentecostals to smells-and-bells-loving Anglicans!—and even more so that women traveled from out of the United States to attend our first "Bible boot camp." One woman came all the way from Europe, where she and her husband had moved to plant a church. As is common with church planting, they weren't exactly received with open arms and pretty much felt like they'd been called to plow cement. So when she heard about the Kerygma Summit on our *Back Porch Theology* podcast, she was compelled by the thought of joining a like-minded sisterhood of Christ followers for the purpose of learning more about God and His Word. She responded quickly to the Holy Spirit's nudge, registered for the event, booked her flight, and before she knew it was flying across the pond to America.

However, when she landed in Chicago en route to Tennessee, she began to have serious doubts. *What in the world was I thinking flying all the way here by myself? I don't know one single person at this event. What if I don't fit in? I don't have any theological training . . . what if one of those seminary professors asks me a question I can't answer—will I look stupid or, worse still, be judged by the other women? Oh my goodness, maybe I should just turn around and go back home.*

Mild anxiety fluttered in her belly as she dutifully boarded the flight to Nashville and found her seat near the back of the plane. Within a few moments, a young woman took the seat next to hers and smiled. Then she asked why the somewhat-anxious church-planting chick was headed to the land of Dollywood and hot chicken:

Perky Stranger: *Are you from Nashville?*

Somewhat-Anxious Church-Planting Chick: *No, I live in Europe—I'm just visiting Nashville for a convention.*

Perky Stranger: *Oh, wow, that's a long way to travel— what kind of convention is it?*

Somewhat-Anxious Church-Planting Chick: *Ummm, well, it's not a convention, per se; I guess it's more like a retreat, and it's not actually in Nashville either. It's in some small town called Franklin.*

Perky Stranger: *Okay, this may sound super random, but are you by chance going to the Kerygma Summit?*

Somewhat-Anxious Church-Planting Chick: *Yes . . . how do you know about Kerygma?*

Perky Stranger: *OH MY GOODNESS, I'M GOING TO KERYGMA TOO! I WORK AT NORTHERN SEMINARY WITH DR. LYNN COHICK, WHO'S ONE OF THE PLENARY SPEAKERS, AND I'M SO EXCITED GOD CONNECTED US LIKE THIS!!!*

By the time they landed in Nashville, the no-longer-anxious church-planting chick and the perky stranger had become fast friends. By the end of the second main session, their story had made it to me, and the no-longer-anxious church-planting chick was given a standing ovation and enveloped in hugs. And by the end of that first Kerygma, that precious church-planting chick had been gifted *thousands* of dollars' worth of Bible translation materials they desperately needed for their church plant across the pond and a long list of phone numbers and emails of new friends committed to help "lift her arms" when she got weary in the wonderful, albeit taxing, work of ministry, like Aaron and Hur did for Moses when he got tired during Israel's battle with the Amalekites (see Exod. 17).

The Trinity isn't a dry, doctrinal concept. Instead, it's the tangible promise of living water for those who find themselves parched with loneliness. It's a friendly boat beaching on the island of isolation. It's the dawn breaking through dark clouds of abandonment. It's a rescuing hand reaching into the scary waters of unplanned solitude. If you're human, you'll come to find it a welcome necessity.

THREE

The Compassionate Authority of King Jesus

Although Christ was God, He took flesh; and having been made man, He remained what He was, God.

Origen

A while ago, we had the undeserved privilege of having Max Lucado on two *Back Porch Theology* podcast episodes. I was so excited to get to sit across the table from dear Max, but I was also a smidge nervous because, while I've known him for twenty-five-plus years (he's even better in person than in print, which is saying a lot), he's one of my heroes of the faith, and I respect him beyond measure.

Unfortunately, my anxious enthusiasm got the best of me, and I yammered on and on and barely gave him a chance to say anything, even though I was supposed to be interviewing HIM! I was embarrassed when those podcasts aired and thought, *Oh my goodness, there I was with a great spiritual leader and instead of gleaning from his wisdom, I gabbed almost incessantly. I might as well have plopped down on a piano bench next to Beethoven and hogged the keyboard with a clunky rendition of "Row, Row, Row Your Boat."*

I can be such a verbose, self-involved woman. And I'm certainly old enough to know better. I was glad to get to see Max again recently when we visited his church in San Antonio and have the chance to apologize in person. But here's how that humble man responded: After giving me a warm hug, he replied sincerely, "Oh, Lisa, that's not at all how I remember our conversation . . . I really enjoyed our time together."

His genuine kindness left me with watery eyes and a grateful heart. I did talk over him and interrupt him frequently—I've got digital proof of my culpability. My idiocy is on the internet for public consumption! Yet Max spends so much time with Jesus, he chooses to focus on what's good in the image bearers around him instead of fixating on their flaws. In this modern era where being canceled, bullied, or shamed is all too common—sometimes it seems to have become a communal blood sport—his deep kindness stood out like a glittering diamond on dark velvet. When someone with well-earned success and authority doesn't live a segregated life in a proverbial ivory tower and instead chooses a humble, compassionate, and accessible way of life, it's remarkable. The fact that the King of all kings did so is astonishing.

Another one of my all-time favorite Christian scholars, saints, and pretend theological boyfriends, Dr. J. I. Packer (whom I had the privilege of meeting in person several years ago and was gobsmacked and garrulous then too!), eloquently elaborated on the astonishing mystery of Jesus's divine authority and incarnate accessibility with this observation:

> The really staggering Christian claim is that Jesus of Nazareth was God made man—that the second person of the Godhead became the "second man" (1 Cor. 15:47), determining human destiny, the second representative head of the race, and that he took humanity without the loss of deity, so that Jesus of Nazareth was as truly divine as he was human.[1]

"He took humanity without the loss of deity . . ." That single phrase of Dr. Packer's quote slays me every time. Our Savior is indeed the King of *all* kings—perfectly powerful and reigning in absolute authority over the entire universe— and yet He chooses to commune with the likes of us in easy-to-reach humility. I was momentarily overwhelmed that a godly man like Max Lucado chose to overlook my bumbling and rambling. I will be forever undone that the Son of God Himself chooses to engage with and envelop mistake-prone yahoos like me.

Taking the Plunge

Way back in 2004, long before middle-aged people began pulling hamstrings while trying to emulate a dance move they saw on social media, an unusual film called *The Passion of the Christ* came to theaters and captured the

---

1. J. I. Packer, *Knowing God* (Downer's Grove, IL: InterVarsity Press, 1973), 53.

imaginations of millions of moviegoers. It grossed over six hundred million dollars with its dramatic portrayal of the life, death, and resurrection of Jesus. The producer, director, and cowriter of this unlikely blockbuster was world-famous Golden Globe and Academy Award winning superstar Mel Gibson. Surprisingly, Mel chose a little-known actor named Jim Caviezel to portray the Messiah in his passion project. And the role ended up making him an overnight sensation. A few months after the movie hit theaters, several of my friends attended a large conference where Christian publishers, record labels, and the then-budding faith-based film industry met with ministry, retail, radio, and television representatives to promote their upcoming projects. Much to their delight, Mr. Caviezel was there in person.

I had dinner with a few of them soon after they got home from the conference and got tickled because all they could talk about was how cute Jim Caviezel was. They couldn't recall any of the new Christian books or worship projects they'd been pitched, but honey, they could describe in great detail the outfits he wore during the three-day conference! At one point, while good-naturedly defending themselves after I teasingly accused them of mild stalking, one of them sighed dreamily and said, "Oh, Lisa, if you'd been there, you would've traipsed after him too because that Jesus was absolutely *gorgeous!*" Even though that took place years ago, all I have to do is say the name Jim Caviezel, and they still swoon!

Now, please hear me, I don't think there's anything wrong with my friends' crush on that hapless actor. But it does provide a practical illustration of how we humans tend to dumb down our Messiah's divinity. It reminds me of something the late, great A. W. Tozer once wrote: "Left to ourselves we tend immediately to reduce God to manageable terms."[2] Although associating our Messiah with an attractive actor isn't really much different than referring to Him by anthropomorphic (which is a fancy seminary word that in the context of theology means using human attributes to describe God) terms like *copilot* or *homeboy* or *the man upstairs*—it's just an easy way to lower the perceived security fence around the King of all kings so that we commoners can access Him. Which isn't necessarily a bad or heretical habit, especially when you consider that a recurring theme in the New Testament is the accessibility of Jesus!

However, we must be careful about how much shine we rub off Jesus's royal crown because when the foundations of our Christian faith were being laid, the undiluted deity of Jesus Christ was (and still is) one of the cornerstones. From the very beginning of the formation of our belief system, the fact that Jesus has a divine nature—that he's really and truly *God* in the flesh—has been nonnegotiable. In fact, the divinity of Jesus was so imperative to orthodoxy that it was the main focus of the first two formal meetings of spiritual bigwigs we talked about in chapter 2, the Council of Nicaea in AD 325 and the Council of Constantinople in AD 381.

Ultimately, those ancient spiritual leaders concluded that Jesus the Son's nature was the exact same nature or substance as God the Father's—the Greek word and theological term for this truism is *homoousios* (in Greek, *homo* means "same," and *ousi* means "substance").

2. A. W. Tozer, *The Knowledge of The Holy: The Attributes of God; Their Meaning in the Christian Life* (San Francisco: HarperOne, 2009), 8.

> From the very beginning of the formation of our belief system, the fact that Jesus has a divine nature—that he's really and truly *God* in the flesh—has been nonnegotiable.

Of course, you know how it is with us Christians; we tend to get in one ditch or another—simply suggest a carpeting color change in the sanctuary and watch the ensuing fireworks!—so about a century after the matter of Jesus's divinity seemed to be conclusively settled at the Council of Nicaea, another formal meeting of Christian leaders had to be convened at the Council of Chalcedon in AD 451 to condemn the "overcorrection" that happened after Nicaea, which was the erroneous assumption some were making that since Jesus was fully divine, He couldn't possibly be fully human at the same time. And the rumblings of what would ultimately congeal to form heresy began to echo through the halls of the early church: *I mean, goodness gracious, how could God Himself shrug into an incarnate suit of skin and hang out with tax collectors and Samaritans without losing some of His deity? Surely all those warm fuzzies Jesus extended were just for the camera, right? How else can you explain it? Our holy Redeemer couldn't be a leper-hugging rabbi at the same time!*

One ancient leader who held this unorthodox view went so far as to insist that when Jesus cried at the tomb of Lazarus, they were faux tears . . . the tears of an actor![3]

---

3. Don Payne, class lecture notes, Biblical and Theological Reflection on the Practice of Ministry, Denver Seminary, July 2019.

Thankfully, the Council of Chalcedon clarified that Jesus Christ has *two* natures and is paradoxically both truly *divine* and truly *human* simultaneously. The theological term for this truism is *hypostasis,* which is the Greek word for "subsistence"—although in the Patristic Era (basically the first five centuries AD), it was used as a technical term for "person," and in modern medical terminology, it refers to the accumulation of fluid or blood in the lower parts of the body or organs under the influence of gravity, such as in the case of poor circulation or after death. So alas, the word *hypostasis* can be a little tricky! And that's why I prefer the two-word term *hypostatic union,* which refers to the supernaturally symbiotic relationship between Jesus's divine and human natures. Jonathan Edwards (one of the key pastors God used to stir up a revival called the Great Awakening in the US in the mid-1700s) brilliantly truncated the hypostatic union as "an admirable conjunction of diverse excellencies."[4] But I think the best explanation comes from the actual creed that was born out of the Council of Chalcedon, which is formally called the Definition of Chalcedon:

> We, then, following the holy fathers, all with one consent teach men to confess one and the same Son, our Lord Jesus Christ, the same perfect in Godhead and also perfect in manhood; truly God and truly man, of a rational soul and body; coessential with the Father according to the Godhead, and consubstantial with us according to the manhood; in all things like unto us, without sin; begotten before all ages of the Father according to the Godhead, and in these

---

[4]. Jonathan Edwards, "The Admirable Conjunction of Diverse Excellencies in Christ Jesus," sermon, 1736.

latter days, for us and for our salvation, born of the Virgin Mary, the mother of God, according to the manhood; one and the same Christ, Son, Lord, Only-begotten, to be acknowledged in two natures, *without confusion, without change, without division, without separation*; the distinction of natures being by no means taken away by the union, but rather the property of each nature being preserved, and concurring in one person and one subsistence, not parted or divided into two persons, but one and the same Son, and only begotten, God the Word, the Lord Jesus Christ; as the prophets from the beginning have declared concerning Him, and the Lord Jesus Christ Himself has taught us, and the creed of the holy fathers has handed down to us.[5]

My mom is an English and grammar buff—she singlehandedly broke my irritating adolescent habit of saying "you know" when I began to tell a story or make an observation by interrupting me with a mischievous grin and the statement, "No, I *don't* know. However, I would very much like for you to tell me!" And one of her biggest pet peeves is when people communicate with negative terminology, so I can almost sense her cringing at the four overt claims of deficiency in the above creed:

1. *Without* confusion
2. *Without* change
3. *Without* division
4. *Without* separation

5. Brian Burns, "The Unity of Jesus' Person," in *Lexham Survey of Theology*, eds. Mark Ward, Jessica Parks, Brannon Ellis, and Todd Hains (Bellingham, WA: Lexham Press, 2018), emphasis mine.

However, since my mom is the one who first introduced me to Jesus, and my hunger for Holy Writ comes directly through her Bible-banging DNA, I know she'll eventually appreciate the liberties those early Christian nonfiction writers took to emphasize all that Jesus is *not*:

1. He's *not* an accidental amalgamation like some divine Frankenstein;
2. He's *not* a diluted version of His former glory prior to the Incarnation;
3. He's *not* a fickle part-time God, part-time human who can't make up His mind; and
4. He's *not* a fragile union like the Beatles who will surely break up!

Granted, that's a lot of information—I think trying to wrap our human cognition around the fact that Jesus is perfectly divine and perfectly human at the same time is more difficult than playing Twister at my age while wearing two pairs of Spanx! But leave it to the illustrious, albeit unassuming, Dr. J. I. Packer to further elucidate the awesome truth of the hypostatic union:

> It is here, in the thing that happened at the first Christmas, that the profoundest and most unfathomable depths of the Christian revelation lie. "The Word became flesh" (John 1:14); God became man; the divine Son became a Jew; the Almighty appeared on earth as a helpless human baby, unable to do more than lie and stare and wriggle and make noises, needing to be fed and changed and taught to talk like any other child. And there was no illusion or

deception in this: the babyhood of the Son of God was a reality. The more you think about it, the more staggering it gets. Nothing in fiction is so fantastic as is the truth of the Incarnation.[6]

The more I think about the King of all kings humbly condescending to wear an ancient pair of Pampers, the more gobsmacked I get! As a rabbi, all Jesus had to do was speak to a raging thunderstorm to make it submit to His majesty (see Matt. 8:23–27). All He had to do was touch a grieving mother's dead son to raise him back to life (see Luke 7:11–17). All He had to do was stroll up to a chaotic scene on a tombstone-strewn hillside, and His presence alone caused an entire troop of the enemy's minions to soil their lying britches (okay, that was a bit of an exegetical stretch, but I really, really hate demons!) because they recognized His deity (see Mark 5:1–13). Yet before Lord Jesus chose to express His supernatural power, He deigned to be potty trained, to be weaned from Mary's milk, to learn Aramaic (the New Testament sayings of Jesus are typically recorded in Greek, but His native tongue was Aramaic—more specifically a Galilean version of western Aramaic—although Luke 4:16–20 reveals that He also read and spoke Hebrew[7]), to do His chores, and to apprentice at the home renovation business of His earthly father, Joe. It's no wonder Dr. Packer enthuses that the Incarnation is more fantastic than any tall tale ever told!

6. Packer, *Knowing God*, 53.
7. Robert H. Stein, *The Method and Message of Jesus' Teachings* (Louisville, KY: Westminster John Knox Press, 1994), 4, 5.

The Significance of Our Savior's Preexistence

The doctrine of Jesus's preexistence as the second person of the Trinity is affirmed in creedal and confessional statements because preexistence is thought to be explicitly present in biblical materials. Jesus's preexistence could be expressed this way: the Son of Mary is the incarnation of the eternal Son of God, who became something that he was not—that is, human—and he was a personal and divine being before he took on flesh.

The significance of Jesus's preexistence is two-fold. First, incarnation and redemption merge. Jesus *comes* from heaven in order to *redeem* his people. In fact, his role as mediator is then retrojected across redemptive history and into creation. If Jesus is God's agent of redemption and creation, then presumably he has always been so. Second, the incarnation was a voluntary act of the Son. It was not forced or imposed. The Son wills to be incarnate, in obedience to the Father, in the power of the Spirit, in order to execute the divine plan for salvation.

Michael Bird, *Evangelical Theology: A Biblical and Systematic Introduction* (Grand Rapids: Zondervan Academic, 2013), 520, 523–24

Finding Treasure in Divine Depths

There are more biblical references to the hypostatic union than there are M&M's in my popcorn at the movies. Which—if you have not yet had the joy of chowing down on hot buttered corn commingled with miniature, melting, candy-coated chocolates at a cinema—is a copious amount! And much like my favorite flavors of Jeni's Ice Cream (sorry, but I've gotten really hungry while researching and writing this chapter), I'm going to have a hard time narrowing it down to only a few. But here goes:

> *The Word* became flesh and dwelt among us. We observed his glory, the glory as *the one and only Son from the Father*, full of grace and truth. (John 1:14 CSB, emphasis mine)

Throughout the New Testament, Jesus is described as the "*Word* of God," and "word" in that familiar description comes from the Greek term *logos* (see, for example, John 1:1). So, in this case, John is clearly pairing the Messiah's incarnate ministry—"[He] became flesh and dwelt among us"—with His divine DNA—"the one and only Son from the Father."

> Pay careful attention to yourselves and to all the flock, in which the Holy Spirit has made you overseers, to care for the *church of God, which he obtained with his own blood*. (Acts 20:28 ESV, emphasis mine)

Don't forget Paul was educated in the law, and you know (sorry, Mom!) how persnickety attorneys can be about verbiage! His connection between the "church of God" and "which he obtained with his own blood"—an obvious reference to the crucifixion of Jesus Christ—is an intentional coupling of Jesus's divine and human natures.

> In your relationships with one another, have the same mindset as Christ Jesus:
>
> > *Who, being in very nature God,*
> > *did not consider equality with God something to be*
> > *used to his own advantage;*

> rather, he made himself nothing
>> by taking the very nature of a servant,
>> being made in human likeness.
> And being found in appearance as a man,
>> he humbled himself
>> by becoming obedient to death—
>>> even death on a cross!
>
> Therefore God exalted him to the highest place
>> and gave him the name that is above every name,
> that at the name of Jesus every knee should bow,
>> in heaven and on earth and under the earth,
> and every tongue acknowledge that Jesus Christ is Lord,
>> to the glory of God the Father. (Phil. 2:5–11, emphasis mine)

I know, I know, this passage is like giving candy (there I go again) to a baby. Well, I suppose, a toddler studying theology, that is! Even a nearsighted squirrel could find the hypostatic-union-of-a-themed nut in this passage.

But just in case you're a bushy-tailed nuisance of a rodent wearing really thick glasses, I will italicize it for you.

> Long ago, at many times and in many ways, God spoke to our fathers by the prophets, but in these last days he has spoken to us by his Son, whom he appointed the heir of all things, through whom also he created the world. He is the radiance of the glory of God *and the exact imprint of his nature*, and he upholds the universe by the word of his power. After making purification for sins, he sat down at the right hand of the Majesty on high, having become as much superior to angels as the name he has

inherited is more excellent than theirs. (Heb. 1:1–4 ESV, emphasis mine)

When we read the author of Hebrews describing our Savior as the "exact imprint" of God's nature in our English Bibles (v. 3), it's helpful to know that *imprint* is translated directly from the Greek word *hypostasis* in the original text—I know, mind blown, right? And finally, the glorious gift of the hypostatic union is why he's also able to describe Jesus as our *empathetic* High Priest:

Therefore, since we have a great high priest who has ascended into heaven, Jesus the Son of God, let us hold firmly to the faith we profess. *For we do not have a high priest who is unable to empathize with our weaknesses, but we have one who has been tempted in every way, just as we are—yet he did not sin.* Let us then approach God's throne of grace with confidence, so that we may receive mercy and find grace to help us in our time of need. (Heb. 4:14–16, emphasis mine)

If we could understand, even in part, that the above passage means our Messiah can legitimately say, "Been there, done that!" with regard to every single emotion in the human continuum—including our deepest grief and most difficult struggles—it would increase our security and decrease our anxiety. Jesus is not some faraway, dispassionate, cape-wearing superhero who redeems us from a distance! Instead, He's an up-close, incarnate, compassionate Savior who intimately relates to every single thing we've been through or are afraid of going through. I firmly believe the juxtaposed miracle of Jesus's *divine humanity* has the power to shift our futures and shape us into a people who somewhat resemble Him.

Leaning into the Shape of Living Water

A year or so after I graduated from college, I flew to California to visit my best friend throughout high school and college, Cindy, and her then-new husband, Peter. We squealed, hugged each other hard, and began telling animated stories while simultaneously plotting where the best and closest Mexican restaurants were so we could fuel our reunion with vats of chips and queso. I can still remember how she was so proud to show me around their little beach bungalow and how the short tour ended in the guest room, where she gleefully gestured to a gift basket that she'd thoughtfully assembled for me. And I can vividly recall the paperback book with a purple cover, titled *Lion and Lamb*, that was flanked by chocolate in the basket. Cindy explained that she knew I already owned the equivalent of a small-town library—she used to tease me about being such a voracious reader—but that she'd been compelled to buy it for me after someone from their young marrieds' Bible study had loaned her a copy to read.

Then she softly added something along the lines of, "Lease, I know you love Jesus with all your heart, but I'm not sure you believe He loves you with all of His, and I think this book can help you." I started reading that little book that evening when I went to bed with my windows open so I could smell the bougainvillea that enveloped their house and hear the Pacific Ocean, which was only a block away, and while I didn't plan on staying up all night—especially after the long, cross-country flight to get there—I found myself so engaged that I ended up finishing the book just as the sun was coming up. It was written by a former Catholic priest (who left the priesthood after falling in love with his wife) and recovering alcoholic named Brennan Manning. He told riveting true stories about the kindness and accessibility of Jesus with more vulnerability than I was used to. His poignant writing made such an impact on me that in the thirty-five-plus years since I first perused *Lion and Lamb*, I've reread it numerous times, along with dozens of other books Brennan Manning (who went to be with Jesus in 2013) wrote.

During the long process of reading through stacks of thick theology tomes in preparation for this *A Jesus-Shaped Life* project, I often found my fingers longingly hovering over the tattered Brennan Manning titles on my bookshelves. I kept telling myself that I didn't have time to read for "pleasure" because I had a deadline to meet. But late one night, I remembered a story from that little purple book of his that was probably my first introduction to the concept of the hypostatic union—not that Mr. Manning used that terminology, of course. Instead, he told an unforgettable true story about a dying man's last embrace:

> The Lion and the Shepherd are one and the same. Ferocious pursuit and unwavering compassion are dual facets of the tremendous Lover who knows not only what hurts us but also how to heal us. And this savage and soothing God is also the Lamb who suffered the pains of death on our behalf. This was the experience of an old man who lay dying. When the priest came to anoint him, he noticed an

empty chair at the man's bedside and asked him who had just been visiting. The sick man replied, "I place Jesus on that chair and I talk to Him." For years, he told the priest, he had found it extremely difficult to pray until a friend explained that prayer was just a matter of talking with Jesus. The friend suggested he imagine Jesus sitting in a chair where he could speak with Him and listen to what He said in reply. "I have had no trouble praying ever since."

Some days later, the daughter of this man came to the parish house to inform the priest that her father had just died. She said, "Because he seemed so content, I left him alone for a couple of hours. When I got back to the room, I found him dead. I noticed a strange thing, though: his head was resting not on the bed but on an empty chair that was beside his bed."

The Lion who will kill all that separates us from Him; the Lamb who was killed to mend that separation—both are symbols and synonyms for Jesus. Relentlessness and tenderness; indivisible aspects of the Divine Reality.[8]

If you haven't yet understood why the *divine humanity* of Jesus matters to you personally, I pray that cleared it up for you. If not, you might want to go ahead and call a cardiologist and schedule an EKG.

---

8. Brennan Manning, *Lion and Lamb: The Relentless Tenderness of Jesus* (Old Tappan, NJ: Chosen Books, 1986), 129–30.

FOUR

As Close as Your Next Breath

> Jesus's resurrection is not mere historical datum; it declares that the Jesus we learn about in the Gospels is now the exalted Lord, who has sent his Spirit so that we may continue to experience his presence.
>
> Craig Keener

I got sick with what I thought was probably the flu the week before Easter 2021, and since I was planning to fly to California a few days later to hang out with some friends, I went to a doctor and got tested for COVID-19. Mind you, I'm not the type who goes to the doctor very often; I'm more of an old-school "take a Tylenol and get over it" kind of girl. But that was back when there was a lot of fear and uncertainty surrounding the pandemic, so I wanted to be extra cautious about the possibility of being infected and thereby putting others at risk. After I tested negative on two separate tests, the doctor assured me that I did not have COVID-19 and that it was only a mild case of bronchitis, which he gave me meds for. Then he assured me there was no problem whatsoever with me traveling to California for a girls' trip. Sometimes I forget it's called the *practice* of medicine because unfortunately he was wrong, and a week later—after coughing my way across the country and back while earnestly explaining to all those accusing sets of eyes glaring at me above their masks that I did *not* have COVID-19, then languishing back at home for several more days, guiltily assuming I'd become a sissy-baby-hypochondriac because it was only a case of mild bronchitis, after all!—I was rushed to the hospital with a very severe case of COVID-19 and COVID-related viral pneumonia.

The first few hours in the hospital were scary because my lung function had become so compromised that it was wreaking havoc on other systems in my body. While waiting to be transferred to a specialized care unit, I overheard two of the medical personnel near me discussing how my case had advanced to the point that excess fluid in my lungs had hardened and become crystallized like shards of glass. One of them said with weary resignation, "Based on how bad her lungs look on the scans, I'm not sure we're going to be able to stabilize her." In defense of those healthcare workers who were risking their own lives in a selfless attempt to save mine, I was so weak I could only lie there with my eyes closed, so I'm sure they thought I was unconscious and unable to hear their candid conversation.

But it was still disconcerting. I was accidentally run over by a car when I was a kid, which fractured my spine in five places and has led to multiple surgeries, including having a titanium plate screwed into my neck to stabilize my cervical vertebrae. Suffice it to say, I'm not a stranger to physical trauma or hospitals. But I'd never been lying in one, listening to caregivers discuss the probability of my death either.

I felt my thoughts drifting to a verse I've heard my mom repeat my whole life: *Absent from the body, present with the Lord* (paraphrase of 2 Cor. 5:8). It's a promise I got to tearfully proclaim at my stepfather's funeral because Dad Angel had sincerely put his hope in Jesus—after a lifetime of stubborn agnosticism—just a few months before his death at eighty-seven.

Absent from the body, present with the Lord. Wow, in a little while I might be stepping into the arms of Jesus. THIS is what perfect peace feels like! Thank You, Jesus . . . thank You, Jesus . . . thank You, Jesus.

I don't know how to describe those brief moments when I thought I was about to meet our Savior face-to-face except for profound serenity. For about sixty solid seconds. Then I experienced emotional whiplash, and my mind began frantically waving its arms toward heaven! I freaked out over the thought of Missy losing another mom and began silently begging God not to let me die yet because I couldn't bear the thought of her being orphaned again.

Wait, God, WAIT! Missy's first mama died when she was a baby, and I'm the only family she has now. She's only eleven years old, God . . . this will break her precious heart into a million pieces, and she probably won't get over losing another mother. Please, please, PLEASE don't take me yet, Father! Please just let Missy grow up a little more, and then You can do whatever You want with me.

Of course, I should've known better. I've been a Christ follower for more than half a century now, and I've always experienced His love and faithfulness to be consistent and unconditional. Plus, *theodicy*—the reality of God's absolute goodness and providence despite the existence of evil and death—is one of my favorite multisyllabic theological terms. Heck, I even did a podcast series about it! I wholeheartedly believe that Romans 8:28—"And we know that in all things God works for the good of those who love him, who have been called according to his purpose"—is true, even when we can't see past the time and space and hardships of humanity to recognize it. But in that moment when I thought about how my physical death would devastate my daughter, the theological reasoning in my head and memory verses in my heart evaporated, and all I was left with was sheer panic about Missy's well-being.

What I deserved was a stern lecture for being so quick to doubt God's sovereign mercy. What I got was the tangible presence of His Spirit. The Holy Spirit flooded the room, and suddenly the only words echoing through my hard head were His.

> *Theodicy*—the reality of God's absolute goodness and providence despite the existence of evil and death.

Honey, I've got her. I love her more than you do, and I promise, I will never, ever leave her. Lisa, whether you live or die, I will love and take care of Missy.

The reassuring voice of God's Spirit was so gentle and kind that I felt my entire body relax in response. And the compassionate blanket He covered my all-too-humanness with left me enveloped by a deep sense of comfort I'd never known before.

There are a gazillion references (okay, maybe that's a slight exaggeration) to the Holy Spirit throughout the Old and New Testaments. They laud how the Spirit of God enables us to confess the true identity of Christ and worship Him (see 1 Cor. 12:3; Eph. 2:18; Phil. 3:3), how He gives believers insight into divine mysteries (see 1 Cor. 2:10), and how He transforms, sanctifies, and shapes us into a more Christlike image (see 1 Cor. 3:16; 2 Cor. 3:18).[1] In light of all those—and many more!—incredible things the Holy Ghost does for God's people, I think it's fitting He's been assigned a bevy of beautiful names in different English Bible translations, including *Helper* in the English Standard Version, *Counselor* in the Christian Standard Bible, and *Advocate* in the New International Version (all of which are translated from the Greek word *paraklētos*, which literally means "called to one's side"). But my all-time favorite name for the Holy Spirit comes from my sweet mom's all-time favorite translation—the King James Version—and that's *Comforter*.

1. Michael A. G. Haykin, "God the Holy Spirit," in *Lexham Survey of Theology*, eds. Mark Ward, Jessica Parks, Brannon Ellis, and Todd Hains (Bellingham, WA: Lexham Press, 2018).

And I will pray the Father, and *he shall give you another Comforter*, that he may abide with you for ever;

Even the Spirit of truth; whom the world cannot receive, because it seeth him not, neither knoweth him: but ye know him; for he dwelleth with you, and shall be in you.

I will not leave you comfortless: I will come to you. (John 14:16–18 KJV, emphasis mine)

Taking the Plunge

Pneumatology is the theological term for the field of study pertaining to Holy Spirit. The term is derived from the Greek word *pneuma*, which means "spirit" or "breath." Which, by the way, is the root word of *pneumonia*. Better yet, for *pneumonologist*, and mine is a great one—although I hope I don't have to see him again anytime soon! But what makes that potentially stodgy-sounding term even better is that the Hebrew word for "spirit" in the Old Testament—*ruach*—is an onomatopoeic term. That means the sound made when saying the word conveys its basic definition—in this case, *the expulsion of wind* or *air in motion*. It's what a cartoonist does by doodling the word "Muah!" above a smooching couple to convey the sound of their kiss. How cool is it that the divinely inscripturated name given Holy Spirit expresses in the most fundamental way that He's the *breath* of life?[2]

Now, before we go any further, you may've noticed I didn't put "the" in front of Holy Spirit in the first sentence

2. Sinclair Ferguson, *The Holy Spirit*, Contours of Christian Theology (Downers Grove, IL: InterVarsity Press, 1996), 16.

of the above paragraph, and I want to assure you it's not an editorial mistake. There's a so-called method to my grammatical madness. My dear Aussie friends Henry and Alex Seeley pastor a vibrant, Bible-believing church here in Nashville called *The Belonging Co*, and several years ago we had a conversation about the Trinity that changed how I usually refer to the third member of the Godhead.

Midway through an animated dinner at their house, when we were all sharing differing theological views and opinions, Henry asked me, "Can you picture the 'faces' of the Trinity?" I was thrown off-balance by his question—as I usually am by good ones—but after thinking about it for a minute or two, I reasoned that since Jesus was incarnate, we have historical proof His biological mom was Jewish, and because I've had the joy of visiting Israel many times, I could probably imagine something close to what He would've looked like as a Middle Eastern man during His earthly ministry. I explained that God the Father's features are fuzzier in my mind, but since Scripture often reveals Him in a paternal context, I imagine His countenance to be that of a regal, ethereal, older gentleman. However, I had to admit that I didn't have a clue how to picture the Holy Spirit since He was, after all, a *spirit*. To which Pastor Henry responded, "Do you think that's why you always put a 'the' in front of His name?"

Up until that very moment, it had never occurred to me how impersonally I addressed Holy Spirit. I don't typically refer to our heavenly Father as "the God"—unless it's followed by "of Abraham, Isaac, and Jacob" or "of mercy" by way of description. And I certainly don't call our Redeemer "the Jesus." Pastor Henry's gentle rebuke made me wonder how much more distance I'd subconsciously put between myself and divine Comfort.

Frankly, it's hard not to get twisted about Him because, like the infamous "church lady" in old Saturday Night Live sketches, the third member of the Trinity is all-too-often caricatured by whatever stream of the church you find yourself swimming in. And even His name—with or without the "the"—prompts us to wrinkle our perplexed brows, according to theologian, pastor, and author Dr. Sinclair Ferguson: "For while his *work* has been recognized, the Spirit *himself* remains to many Christians an anonymous, faceless aspect of the divine being. Even the title 'Holy Spirit' evokes a different gamut of emotions from those expressed in response to the titles of 'Father' and 'Son.'"[3]

Of course, there's a whole other colorful reason to wrinkle your brows in confusion—worse still, belittle people whose pneumatology differs from your own—because one of the most well-known yet hotly debated gifts attributed to the Holy Spirit is *speaking in tongues* (from the Greek word *glossolalia*—*glóssa* means "tongue" and *lalia* means "talking"), which we read about in Acts 2:

> When the day of Pentecost came, they were all together in one place. Suddenly a sound like the blowing of a violent wind came from heaven and filled the whole house where they were sitting. They saw what seemed to be tongues of fire that separated and came to rest on each of them. All of them were filled with the Holy Spirit and began to *speak in other tongues as the Spirit enabled them*. (vv. 1–4, emphasis mine)

3. Ferguson, *Holy Spirit*, 12.

Immediately following the disciples' Spirit-given ability to speak in other tongues, Luke clarifies that the huge crowd of Jews who'd gathered in Jerusalem to celebrate Pentecost (which was kind of like an ancient Super Bowl or a World Cup or a Mardi Gras or a Buc-ee's grand opening) from at least fifteen different nations—therefore speaking at least fifteen different dialects or languages!—understood *exactly* what the disciples were saying:

> Now there were staying in Jerusalem God-fearing Jews from every nation under heaven. *When they heard this sound, a crowd came together in bewilderment, because each one heard their own language being spoken. Utterly amazed, they asked: "Aren't all these who are speaking Galileans? Then how is it that each of us hears them in our native language?* Parthians, Medes and Elamites; residents of Mesopotamia, Judea and Cappadocia, Pontus and Asia, Phrygia and Pamphylia, Egypt and the parts of Libya near Cyrene; visitors from Rome (both Jews and converts to Judaism); Cretans and Arabs—*we hear them declaring the wonders of God in our own tongues!*" Amazed and perplexed, they asked one another, "What does this mean?" (vv. 5–12, emphasis mine)

The ethnic barriers that likely existed at the beginning of this international gathering quickly dissipated when the disciples were filled with the power of Holy Spirit and spoke in tongues because it was also a miraculous moment of *xenoglossia* (*xenos* is the Greek word for "foreigner" and *glóssa* is the Greek word for "tongue" or "language"), which means the words that sounded strange to the disciples as they were vocalizing them were heard and comprehended by that crowd of foreigners in their native language! As a result, thousands put their hope in the recently resurrected Jesus, and His two declarative promises from Acts 1 were fulfilled with jaw-dropping immediacy:

> But you will receive power when the Holy Spirit has come upon you, and you will be my witnesses in Jerusalem and in all Judea and Samaria, and to the end of the earth. (Acts 1:8 ESV, emphasis mine)

Unfortunately, that phenomenal event in biblical history has also led to much discord and consternation among Christians because some brilliant theologians, wonderful pastors, Christian leaders, and committed Christ followers believe the only proper manifestation of tongues was when it occurred as *xenolalia*—a known language—as it occurred at the biblical event of Pentecost in the book of Acts. Therefore, they reason that it is no longer a valid sign or gift of Holy Spirit. The theological term for that doctrinal viewpoint is *cessationist*, because it asserts that supernatural tongues have ceased. There are scads of other brilliant theologians, wonderful pastors, Christian leaders, and committed Christ followers who believe that speaking in tongues is a relevant spiritual gift and think *xenolalia* occurred again after the phenomenon in Acts and still occurs in modern culture. Still other brilliant theologians, wonderful pastors, Christian leaders, and committed Christ followers are passionate that *glossolalia*—aka ecstatic speech that is not heard or comprehended as a known language—is a valid outward manifestation of the inward presence of Holy Spirit and is helpful for their private devotional experience, spiritual growth, and evangelistic zeal. Some of those same self-described "charismatic" or "Pentecostal" Christians also believe that speaking in tongues should be practiced in corporate worship settings when accompanied by a separate, prophetic "interpretation" to encourage the entire church.

And those are just a *few* of the *many* dissenting views of that *one* gift from Holy Spirit!

The very real and present danger regarding the dramatically different Christian viewpoints on speaking in tongues isn't just that it can cause division, confusion, and elitism in the body of Christ, it's that it tends to make us forget about *all the other gifts* that are ours through God's indwelling Spirit. Awesome stuff like love, joy, peace, patience, kindness, goodness, faithfulness, gentleness, and self-control (see Gal. 5:22–23). Furthermore, as the following passages will prove, the Spirit of God *empowers, purifies, teaches, comforts, convicts, and guides Christ followers*—so whatever your personal understanding is regarding the gift of tongues and whether or not you can picture Holy Spirit in your mind's eye, He's someone you definitely want to get closer to!

Finding Treasure in Divine Depths

Although that party at Pentecost is probably the most familiar passage that includes the third member of the Trinity by name, He's been around from the beginning. In fact, that exact moniker—*Holy Spirit*—is mentioned three times in the Old Testament. First when David—the teenage slingshot sensation who went on to become the second king of Israel—begged Holy Spirit not to leave him after he got busted getting jiggy with Bathsheba while she was still married to Uriah the Hittite:

> Create in me a pure heart, O God,
>   and renew a steadfast spirit within me.
> Do not cast me from your presence
>   or take your *Holy Spirit* from me. (Ps. 51:10–11, emphasis mine)

And then again when the prophet Isaiah laments the consequences of Israel's rebellion:

> Yet they rebelled
>   and grieved his *Holy Spirit*.
> So he turned and became their enemy
>   and he himself fought against them.
>
> Then his people recalled the days of old,
>   the days of Moses and his people—
> where is he who brought them through the sea,
>   with the shepherd of his flock?
> Where is he who set
>   his *Holy Spirit* among them? (Isa. 63:10–11, emphasis mine)

But I like to think His favorite nicknames in the Old Testament are "the Spirit of God," "the Spirit of the Lord," "Spirit of the Living God," and "My Spirit" because those are sprinkled more liberally throughout it, such as in the very beginning, when He was actively present in Creation:

> The earth was empty and had no form. Darkness covered the ocean, and ==God's Spirit was moving== over the water. (Gen. 1:2 NCV, emphasis mine)

Or when He mediated between Moses and the Israelites in the wilderness:

> Now two men remained in the camp, one named Eldad, and the other named Medad, and the Spirit rested on them. They were among those registered, but they had not gone out to the tent, and so they prophesied in the camp. And a young man ran and told Moses, "Eldad and Medad are prophesying in the camp." And Joshua the son of Nun, the assistant of Moses from his youth, said, "My lord Moses, stop them." But Moses said to him, "Are you jealous for my sake? Would that all the LORD's people were prophets, that the LORD would put *his Spirit* on them!" (Num. 11:26–29 ESV, emphasis mine)

Further on in the Psalter (all 150 psalms were originally written as songs, so I like to think of that wonderful book in the middle of the Bible as God's playlist), David raves about the comfort he receives from the constant companionship of Holy Spirit:

> Is there any place I can go to avoid *your Spirit*?
>   to be out of your sight?
> If I climb to the sky, you're there!
>   If I go underground, you're there!
> If I flew on morning's wings
>   to the far western horizon,
> You'd find me in a minute—

> you're already there waiting!
> Then I said to myself, "Oh, he even sees me in the
> dark!
> At night I'm immersed in the light!"
> It's a fact: darkness isn't dark to you;
> night and day, darkness and light, they're all the
> same to you. (Ps. 139:7–12 MSG, emphasis
> mine)

Holy Spirit gets even more press in the New Testament. Basically, once Jesus is resurrected then ascends into heaven to sit at the right hand of God the Father, the rest of biblical history becomes His highlight reel! But the one I'd like us to watch in slow motion multiple times occurs in Paul's letter to the Romans:

> For all who are led by the Spirit of God are sons of God. For you did not receive the spirit of slavery to fall back into fear, but you have received the spirit of sonship. When we cry, "Abba! Father!" . . . (Rom. 8:14–15 RSV)

Even though "spirit of sonship" (also translated "spirit of adoption") is only used this one time in Scripture to describe Holy Spirit, ancient church father John Calvin insisted that it should be His *title*![4] And I have to agree, because His constant reminder that I get to call the Creator of the Universe "Dad" herds my prone-to-wander heart back toward the flock of the Good Shepherd on a regular basis.

---

4. John Calvin, *Institutes*, 3.1.3.

> ## Closer than Your Next Breath
>
> Irenaeus of Lyons (ca. 200) claims to be acquainted with the phenomenon of tongues, although his report is succinct: "We have heard many brethren in the church having prophetic gifts and speaking through the spirit in all tongues and bringing to light men's secrets for the common good and explaining the mysteries of God. Such persons the apostle calls spiritual."
>
> John Calvin is sometimes called "the theologian of the Holy Spirit" based on his emphasis on the Holy Spirit's role in union with Christ, sanctification, the sacraments, and every aspect of the *ordo salutis* (which is Latin for "the order of salvation").
>
> The baptismal formula of Matthew 28:19 contains an initial and succinct point of departure in this discussion. Here, God is described as "Father, Son, and Holy Spirit." Since this baptismal formula implies a radical, wholehearted commitment to God, Christian authors in the New Testament and in the ancient church naturally included the Holy Spirit within the Godhead.
>
> _{Luke Timothy Johnson, "Tongues, Gift of," in *The Anchor Yale Bible Dictionary*, ed. David Noel Freedman (New York: Doubleday, 1992), 6:598–99; Kelly M. Kapic and Wesley Vander Lugt, "Holy Spirit," in *Pocket Dictionary of the Reformed Tradition*, The IVP Pocket Reference Series (Downers Grove, IL: IVP Academic, 2013), 87; Haykin, "God the Holy Spirit"}

Leaning into the Shape of Living Water

I'm sure you've heard the following preincarnate passage from Luke's Gospel as many times as I've asked for another basket of chips at a Tex-Mex restaurant, but please bear with me and peruse it one more time:

> Gabriel appeared to [Mary] and said, "Greetings, favored woman! The Lord is with you!"

Confused and disturbed, Mary tried to think what the angel could mean. "Don't be afraid, Mary," the angel told her, "for you have found favor with God! You will conceive and give birth to a son, and you will name him Jesus. He will be very great and will be called the Son of the Most High. The Lord God will give him the throne of his ancestor David. And he will reign over Israel forever; his Kingdom will never end!"

Mary asked the angel, "But how can this happen? I am a virgin."

The angel replied, *"The Holy Spirit will come upon you, and the power of the Most High will overshadow you. So the baby to be born will be holy, and he will be called the Son of God."* (Luke 1:28–35 NLT, emphasis mine)

Before I get to the point, may I remind you that Christianity isn't the only ancient literature that includes some type of "virgin" birth story? If you can remember that Greek mythology course you took in college, it was replete with scintillating tall tales about human women becoming pregnant after having sexual intercourse with one of the "gods" of the pantheon and then giving birth. Those ancient fables are where we find the fictional births of Perseus and Hercules and, ultimately, Wonder Woman (whose recent movies starring Gal Gadot I thoroughly enjoyed because I watched them while noshing on a tub of hot popcorn laced with gooey M&M's!).

The notable disparity between Jesus's actual birth narrative and these false pagan narratives is the lack of sexual intercourse. Or abuse. Because Greek mythology describes Zeus as a serial philanderer and rapist who had dozens of affairs, mistresses, and illegitimate children through the ages. All of which stands in stark contrast to the gentle, even *gentlemanly*, way the angel Gabriel greets Mary and then gives her a peek at the miraculous sonogram in her future.

And to make this oh-so-important point about the chaste—albeit *powerful*—genesis of Mary's pregnancy even more clear, the original Greek word Luke uses to describe how the Holy Spirit would "come upon" her in verse 35 is *eperchomai*, a Greek word that means "to draw near." It's the exact same word used at the beginning of Acts, when Jesus promises His followers that Holy Spirit is coming, right before He ascends into heaven to sit at the right hand of God the Father:[5]

> While he was with them, he commanded them not to leave Jerusalem, but to wait for the Father's promise. "Which," he said, "you have heard me speak about; for John baptized with water, but you will be baptized with the Holy Spirit in a few days."
>
> So when they had come together, they asked him, "Lord, are you restoring the kingdom to Israel at this time?"
>
> He said to them, "It is not for you to know times or periods that the Father has set by his own authority. But you will receive power *when the Holy Spirit has come on you*, and you will be my witnesses in Jerusalem, in all Judea and Samaria, and to the ends of the earth." (Acts 1:4–8 CSB, emphasis mine)

Here's the point: The young woman God chose to carry the incarnation didn't have sex with a man, much less Holy

---

5. J. Reiling and J. L. Swellengrebel, *A Handbook on the Gospel of Luke*, UBS Handbook Series (New York: United Bible Societies, 1993), 59.

Spirit, because her pregnancy wasn't biological. Instead, *the Spirit of God brought something out of nothing*. And when Holy Spirit "came upon" the disciples in Acts and empowered them to speak eloquently in languages *they'd never even heard before* so they could clearly proclaim the good news of Jesus Christ to foreigners, He wasn't dealing with dudes who had any special aptitude for linguistics. Instead, most of those men came from blue-collar backgrounds, which in ancient semitic culture meant they were illiterate (except for maybe Matt, who had an accounting background before becoming a disciple, and Paul, who went to law school—but he wasn't a Christ follower yet at that particular Pentecost, so he doesn't count). Once again, *the Spirit of God brought something out of nothing*.

Birth from barrenness. Clarity from chaos. Vibrancy out of void.

A few days after I was admitted to the hospital with COVID-19 and my condition had vastly improved, a physician walked into my room and told me he'd just found out I was a vocational Bible teacher. Then he very compassionately, albeit soberly, explained that because of how much damage my lungs had sustained, they probably wouldn't be able to retain more than two or three minutes of residual oxygen. That I would likely be tethered to a portable oxygen tank for the foreseeable future. That I would probably never again be able to project my voice like I used to. He gently encouraged me to focus on the fact that I'd survived, that I was going home to Missy, but said not to hold out false hope that I would be able to "preach" again.

My voice was barely discernible when I tried to thank him for being the tool God used to save my life. Then I wheezed, "Doc, do you know what the Greek word in the New Testament is for *spirit*?" Of course, he looked at me like I had three heads. But I knew he knew the word because he's a *pneumonologist*, and he's a committed Christ follower. I had just enough residual air left to whisper the answer to my own question when he didn't.

"It means breath, Doc. Holy Spirit is my BREATH. And with all due respect, sir, if He wants me to keep telling stories about how much Jesus loves us, He'll give me the power to do so."

A few months later, after taking multiple tests to assess how my lungs were healing, that same dear man walked into the exam room where I was waiting and said with a smile, "Lisa, I don't use the word *miracle* very often, but that's the only way I can explain how your lung function is already ninety percent of what it used to be. You may not be able to climb Everest anytime soon, but you can preach!"

Even Jesus didn't self-resuscitate. Remember Paul's words from Romans 8:11: "*If the Spirit of him who raised Jesus from the dead* dwells in you, he who raised Christ Jesus from the dead will also give life to your mortal bodies through his Spirit who dwells in you" (ESV, emphasis mine; see also 1 Pet. 3:18). So, if you feel like you're at the very end of your rope . . . like your heart is completely out of breath, then be encouraged because you're at the exact point of deprivation where Holy Spirit gives mouth-to-mouth resuscitation!

FIVE

The Calibration of Christlikeness

> Biblical orthodoxy without compassion is surely the ugliest thing in the world.
>
> Francis Schaeffer

When I got out of the hospital after that COVID scare a few years ago, I transitioned into a brief flurry of activity that my nephew John Michael—who lived with us at the time—now teasingly refers to as my *signs of life* era. I was just so incredibly grateful to be alive that I went on a wee buying spree. I bought two big cherry trees from a fancy-schmancy nursery. After which I bought new Adirondack chairs from which I could sit and gaze at the copious, pink blooms of the cherry trees because I think they're such beautiful reminders of how every spring God brings colorful new life out of the drab, brown dormancy of winter. Then I bought lots of accoutrements for outdoor grilling because I envisioned eating yummy barbecued chicken and cheeseburgers and buttery corn on the cob and bacon-wrapped jalapeños stuffed with cream cheese (Missy was not wearing her navy-blue school uniform shirt in this particular vision) while sitting in those low, wide chairs and gazing at the copious, pink blooms of my new prized cherry trees.

Mind you, I didn't stop to consider how I was still so weak physically that my oh-so-patient nephew would be the one who'd have to wrestle those heavy trees into our little "dump" trailer (we live out in the boonies where there's no trash pickup, so we regularly tote bags of trash to the dump ourselves), dig two massive holes in our rocky soil to plant them, *and* be the one who assembled the 912 loose parts for those chairs and all the barbecuing paraphernalia. Poor thing began to act like a long-tailed cat in a room full of rocking chairs every time a delivery truck pulled up the driveway!

I also didn't consider how fast all the calories I gobbled during those gleeful "I'm so grateful to be alive" weeks would add up, given the fact that I wasn't yet able to exercise like I normally did. Before I knew it, my belly was blooming more than the cherry trees. And while my post-hospitalization respiratory-function tests revealed miraculous healing in my lungs, I also had to have follow-up blood work with my "regular" physician, which revealed elevated cholesterol and blood sugar levels. Not to mention, my middle-aged-lady, spandex-infused jeans had gotten to the zipper-is-about-to-pull-apart point!

So, I made one more expensive purchase—a pair of super cute running shoes—and started moving again. It took a long time, but eventually I bid farewell to sixty-five stubborn pounds, got my cholesterol and blood sugar back into the healthy range, and got rid of my stretchy pants. The problem was (isn't it crazy how we tend to careen from one ditch to another?), now I had lots of stretchy *skin*! Which led to yet another medical malady that summer when I was carrying big stones across our five-acre farmette for yet another landscaping project (John Michael had wisely moved into an apartment for his own physical health), and I reasoned to myself, "Since I have to tote these heavy rocks anyway, I might as well turn this into an arm workout to firm up the wobbly bits around my armpits." And I tried to toss an especially large one over my head, which resulted in a very loud ripping noise. I thought, *Uh-oh. I think I just broke one of my wobbly bits.* Turns out it was the sound of my left bicep, left rotator cuff, and left labrum cussing and screaming in unison, "You're way too old to be hurling boulders, lady!"

I ended up back in the hospital for a surgery to repair my torn rotator cuff and labrum, as well as to have two holes drilled in my humerus bone through which they used a screw (which on my X-ray looks exactly like a drywall screw from Home Depot, so I'm not sure why it was so expensive) to reattach my repaired bicep. And now—months after the surgery—my hair still looks like I've been riding in the back of a truck since I still can't use a blow-dryer with my left arm because I have an impinged nerve. According to the orthopedist, something hasn't aligned quite right in my now nearly bionic shoulder, and until those internal parts are working in tandem again, I won't be able to fix my hair, fasten my bra strap (which is another story, completely unsuitable for a book on theology), or sleep comfortably at night.

I'm learning the wincing way how necessary *physical alignment*—that is, the proper adjustment and/or balance of components for coordinated functioning—is for me to have a strong body (and halfway decent hair!). More importantly, God has been trying to teach me for a long time how necessary *spiritual alignment*—that is, the proper adjustment and/or balance of our *orthodoxy, orthopraxy,* and *orthopathy*—is to have a strong soul. *Ortho* is a Greek prefix that means "right" or "correct," and

- *dox* means "belief"—therefore in the Christian context, the word *orthodoxy* refers to the "right beliefs" about God;
- *praxis* means "activity"—therefore in the Christian context, the word *orthopraxy* refers to the "right actions" in light of what we believe to be true about God; and
- *páthos* means "feelings" or "emotion"—therefore in the Christian context, the word *orthopathy* refers to the "right feelings" in light of what we believe to be true about God.

I spent a good deal of time in my twenties and thirties riding and racing mountain bikes, and one of the first things you need to learn when attempting to hurtle down a narrow rocky trail on two knobby wheels is *flow*. Your biology and the bike's machinery have to be synergistic or else you're going to leave more blood on the trail and spend more time

> ### What's the Posture of Your Heart?
>
> *Praxis* might initially sound like just a fancy term for "practice" but there's a significant difference between the two words. Because unlike *practice*, which can describe rote behavior like practicing one's multiplication tables or parallel parking skills, *praxis* refers to an action in which there is inherent meaning that reflects the motive of one's heart. *Praxis* is a term taken directly from the Greek, literally meaning "deed, action or activity." The basis for its contemporary use lies in two ideas: first, theoretical reflection arises out of active commitment, and therefore the criterion for right thinking/belief (orthodoxy) is right action/behavior (orthopraxy); second, in turn, the goal of right thinking/belief is the transformation of the world. Praxis denotes the kind of active commitment that leads to theoretical reflection. The use of praxis in this sense seeks to bring about the uniting of, or the overcoming of, such conceptual dualities as theory and practice, belief and action, or commitment and its ethical outworking. For example, giving a gift for the sole reason of getting something back in return isn't giving a "gift" because by definition a gift is free.
>
> Stanley J. Grenz and Jay T. Smith, *Pocket Dictionary of Ethics*, The IVP Pocket Reference Series (Downers Grove, IL: InterVarsity Press, 2003), 94; Don Payne, class syllabus and teaching notes, Biblical and Theological Reflection on the Practice of Ministry, Denver Seminary, July 2019

in the ER than you bargained for. And believe me, I have the gnarly scars to prove that it took me a long time to learn how to coordinate my body with a bike. If only someone had encouraged me to cocoon myself in Bubble Wrap when I started the sport! This next section is kind of like Bubble Wrap for the walk of faith, y'all—it'll help us learn how to synergize our orthodoxy, orthopraxy, and orthopathy so we don't go careening off the path of Christian living and land in a bloody heap of hypocrisy or hopelessness!

Taking the Plunge

I've had so many aha moments in the doctoral program at Denver Seminary that I wish there was an emoji of a saucer-eyed middle-aged chick with the caption, "WOW!" And my first class—Biblical and Theological Reflection on the Practice of Ministry—with Dr. Jim Howard (who's since become a spiritual mentor, thesis adviser, podcast teammate, and perennially teasing big brother of sorts) and Dr. Don Payne (the current provost of Denver Seminary, whom I have the utmost respect for) was a long, unremitting *WOW*. They're both so brilliant that I often found myself typing notes so fast and furious on my laptop that my hands would cramp, yet they're also so engaging that I'd find myself perched on the edge of my seat, waiting expectantly for what they'd say next (remember the whole "theology isn't boring" theme of chapter one?). In fact, I almost fell out of my seat on the first day of class when they explained the difference between formal theology and functional theology!

Here's the deal: Most Christians have two theologies. We have a "formal theology," which could be loosely described as the statement of faith that hangs in our church foyer or is written on their website. If your church includes liturgy in worship, it might also be expressed in a corporate confession like the Apostles' Creed. It's how we would answer the question—provided it's posed by someone who truly wants to know—"What are your personal beliefs about God and spirituality?" It's pretty much a layman's term for *orthodoxy* (right beliefs about God). On the other hand, our "functional theology" is how we live our everyday lives when we're *not* worshiping in church or in a Christ-centered small group or attending a Christian concert or faith-based event. It's pretty much a layman's term for *orthopraxy* and *orthopathy* (how we live, act, and feel in light of what we believe to be true about God). Although our formal theology and our functional theology are not synonymous, they should certainly overlap. And the areas where they don't overlap are seedbeds of hypocrisy. *Because if what we believe to be true of God doesn't change the shape of our heart and how we live our lives, then it's simply a conceptual idea.*[1]

And that's the part where I almost committed the very unladylike act of sliding out of my chair in the middle of class. Because knowledge—conceptual ideas or cognitive information—is a bunch of fig leaves I've often used to camouflage fear and shame. I became a Christ follower as a little girl, not long after I was first sexually molested, so unfortunately the visceral feelings of being dirty and damaged were intertwined with hearing preachers with booming voices and bulging neck veins yell about how all humans were sinners who needed the blood of Jesus to cleanse our filthy hearts. Unfortunately, the resulting amalgamation of "my body is dirty because I've been molested" and "my heart is dirty because I'm a sinner" helped mold me into a smiling-on-the-outside-but-wary-on-the-inside, self-protective performer. I learned to quickly read a room and figure out

---

1. Jim Howard and Don Payne, class syllabus and teaching notes, Biblical and Theological Reflection on the Practice of Ministry, Denver Seminary, July 2019.

who the potentially dangerous people were, then be quick on my feet when it came to reciting a Bible passage or telling a funny story to entertain them so I'd be less likely to be pulled into a dark closet. The abuse continued well into my adolescence, and by the time I was old enough to protect myself, I didn't know how to shift my mind out of its vigilante role. Trust didn't come easily for me, with regard to both other people's intentions and my own emotional vulnerability, because all too often, whoever I trusted with my heart either lied, left, or filleted it.

Compounding my penchant for facade was the fact that one of my abusers was a well-known leader in a local church. Then, when I was a teenager, a senior pastor whom I deeply admired was discovered to be in a long-term affair with a lady who led Bible studies in our congregation. For a young woman like me who was devoted to all things Jesus and His church, the news was devastating. Obviously, I hadn't heard the terms *formal theology* or *functional theology* yet, but I'd seen more than my young stomach could handle of hypocrisy. So I subconsciously resolved to remain dutiful to matters of the Christian faith yet keep my heart safely locked away from all the drama and deceit. I wish this declaration by Dr. Bruce Demarest didn't resonate so much with me: "My evangelical culture and training led me to this belief: Personal experience is an untrustworthy pillar for Christian faith and life. Therefore, you should relegate life and matters of the heart to an inferior place."[2]

It wasn't until I had a panic attack while teaching a Bible study in my forties that I began to do the really hard work of

2. Demarest, *Satisfy Your Soul*, 25.

identifying the segregate facets of my faith—what I believed to be true of God, how I lived in light of those beliefs, and the oft fearful and fickle feelings that marble the meat of my faith—so as to unify them. I was about halfway through a thirty-minute message to a lovely group of women, which included many dear friends, when my heart began to beat wildly and I began to sweat profusely. And I don't mean a glowing sheen of perspiration like athletic models wear either. I mean rivulets running down my face, soaking my shirt and the seat of my pants. I tried to continue speaking and acting casually, as if it was totally normal for my body to spurt in public, but inwardly I worried, *Uh-oh, I think Reader's Digest listed this as the sign of an impending heart attack. But I'm pretty sure it said you'd also have a tingling sensation in your right arm if it was a heart attack. Or maybe it was the left arm? Oh, crud, I really don't want to have a heart attack right here, right now.*

After rambling and leaking for several more awkward minutes and feeling completely disassociated with my body, as if I were floating a few feet away, I watched a friend in the crowd frown, lean over to another woman, and whisper, "Is she okay?" in blurry slow motion. It was all I could do not to scream, "NO, I'm not!" and collapse into a puddle of tears. Instead, I stammered a benediction and stumbled off the stage. As soon as I got into my car, I called a counselor and made the first appointment of what turned into over two decades of digging because when you've become a master faker like I had, the truth gets buried very deep. And while I believe all the answers to life's questions can be found in God's Word, I've also come to realize that I need the help of those much wiser than me to find them and apply their healing balm to the darkest bruises of my heart. I needed serious triage before Holy Spirit could weave the raveling threads of orthodoxy, orthopraxy, and orthopathy into a tapestry of authentic faith.

Finding Treasure in Divine Depths

There are so many passages that illustrate and extol the alignment of our beliefs, actions, and emotions as God's people, but we're just going to peruse two: one in the Old Testament and one in the New Testament, one affirmation and one admonition. Let's start with the good news, but before we dive in, I should qualify that it might sound like bad news at first because it's one of the saddest songs in the Psalter. John Calvin said it well when he described the Psalms as "an anatomy of all parts of the soul"[3] because they record both the weeping and the dancing of God's people—the rapture and rupture of *real* life:

> As the deer pants for streams of water,
>   so my soul pants for you, my God.
> My soul thirsts for God, for the living God.
>   When can I go and meet with God? (Ps. 42:1–2)

Since water is used as a metaphor for God's grace throughout the Bible, I think it's fitting that the Sons of Korah (the ancient worship leaders who wrote this sacred song) use thirst here at the beginning of their bluesy tune to underscore how only God can quench the parched heart

---

3. John Calvin, *Commentary on the Book of Psalms*, vol. 1 (Grand Rapids: Eerdmans, 1949), xxxvii.

of despair. But then the whole liquid theme starts running downhill straight to self-indulgent city:

> My tears have been my food
>   day and night,
> while people say to me all day long,
>   "Where is your God?"
> These things I remember
>   as I pour out my soul:
> how I used to go to the house of God
>   under the protection of the Mighty One
> with shouts of joy and praise
>   among the festive throng. (vv. 3–4)

Their fretting stops for a brief moment when they refocus on their Redeemer:

> Why, my soul, are you downcast?
>   Why so disturbed within me?
> Put your hope in God,
>   for I will yet praise him,
>   *my Savior and my God.* (v. 5, emphasis mine)

But regrettably, just as most of us are guilty of doing from time to time, they regress to the naval-gazing posture of victimhood:

> My soul is downcast within me;
>   therefore I will remember you
> from the land of the Jordan,
>   the heights of Hermon—from Mount Mizar.
> Deep calls to deep

> in the roar of your waterfalls;
> all your waves and breakers
>   have swept over me. (vv. 6–7)

The Sons of Korah originated from the tribe of Levi and were given the task of leading worship through music (1 Chron. 6:16, 31–48; 2 Chron. 20:19) in the tent of meeting—which was where the Israelites worshiped before they had a brick-and-mortar building—and then in the temple when it was constructed. And these particular lyrics express melancholy nostalgia about their former glory, when they had the platform and purpose (and surely lots of attention and admiration) of leading an ancient choir of God's people.

I turned sixty-one recently, and along with discounts at fast-food restaurants, six-plus decades of life have earned me some well-worn perspective. Here's what I've learned the hard way about nostalgia—be careful about taking field trips to your past because, unless Holy Spirit is driving the bus, you're likely to end up in a sinkhole!

Fortunately, these pensive hymn writers finally stop pining for the past and remember why they can hang on to hope smack-dab in the middle of their current disappointment. It's as if they pinch themselves back to reality and exclaim, "Oh yeah! Now we remember how Yahweh said He would *never* leave or forsake us, no matter what!"

> By day the LORD directs his love,
>   at night his song is with me—
>   a prayer to the God of my life.
>
> I say to God my Rock,
>   "Why have you forgotten me?

> Why must I go about mourning,
>   oppressed by the enemy?"
> My bones suffer mortal agony
>   as my foes taunt me,
> saying to me all day long,
>   "Where is your God?"
>
> *Why, my soul, are you downcast?*
>   *Why so disturbed within me?*
> *Put your hope in God,*
>   *for I will yet praise him,*
>   *my Savior and my God.* (vv. 8–11, emphasis mine)

Psalm 42 concludes by repeating the restorative question in verse 5 (which is also repeated in Ps. 43; therefore some scholars think it isn't a separate psalm but instead another part of Ps. 42), and I so appreciate the affirmative ending—as a matter of fact, all of the psalms of lament end with something redemptive, except for Psalm 88, which ends with what I like to call carb-restricted-diet kind of prose: "darkness is my closest friend." However, what I appreciate most about psalms of lament like this (*lament* is the formal classification for the "sad" psalms) is that God allowed them to be included in His hymnal in the first place.

Instead of disowning disillusioned people, God offers us the *fifty-nine* psalms of lament like an engraved invitation to express our sorrow. To be honest when our hearts are left or lied to or filleted and not plaster fake happy faces over our sad feelings or try to pull ourselves up by our bootstraps. What a glorious relief that our Creator Redeemer doesn't expect us to curate our emotions and only bring the ones before Him that are perfectly congruent with an ancient

Christian creed or our church's statement of faith. Instead, God lovingly invites us to bring *everything*—our heartbreak, disappointment, and even our whining—to Him as an act of worship. Frankly, since the majority shareholders of the Psalter are sad songs, it would seem being honest about the hard stuff in our lives is about as biblically orthodox as you can get!

Now let's get to that New Testament passage that highlights the lack of spiritual alignment. It's found toward the end of Matthew's Gospel, in chapter 23. Please read the entire chapter when you have time, but for now we'll just look at two of the "woes" in this passage that is often referred to as "the seven woes":

> Woe to you, teachers of the law and Pharisees, you hypocrites! You clean the outside of the cup and dish, but inside they are full of greed and self-indulgence. Blind Pharisee! First clean the inside of the cup and dish, and then the outside also will be clean.
>
> Woe to you, teachers of the law and Pharisees, you hypocrites! You are like whitewashed tombs, which look beautiful on the outside but on the inside are full of the bones of the dead and everything unclean. In the same way, on the outside you appear to people as righteous but on the inside you are full of hypocrisy and wickedness. (vv. 25–28)

God lovingly invites us to bring *everything*— our heartbreak, disappointment, and even our whining—to Him as an act of worship.

The majority of Jewish people during the time period of Jesus's earthly ministry were just regular blue-collar folks trying to eke out a living as farmers or shepherds. The Hebrew term for those everyday people is *am ha'aretz*, which literally means "people of the land."[4] Most men, women, and children among the *am ha'aretz* didn't have the luxury of a formal education and were illiterate. Therefore, since they couldn't read Torah for themselves, they had to trust the Pharisees, who were an educated sect of Jewish men who were influential from around 150 BC until AD 135 (the origin of the term *Pharisee* comes from an Aramaic word that means "to separate" or "divide"), to interpret it for them.

Based on biblical narrative, some of those Pharisees (it's important to note that not all Pharisees were demeaning, divisive, or disingenuous; Nicodemus and Joseph of Arimathea were both Pharisees, and they are portrayed positively in the Gospels) were like overzealous school crossing guards with giant whistles when it came to being the liaisons between the Jewish people and God because they were persnickety about applying Torah (the first of three divisions of the Hebrew Scriptures, which is now part of our Old Testament canon) to every single facet of life. They spent inordinate amounts of time hunched over copies of the Mosaic law in order to codify six-hundred-plus biblical imperatives. Then they used their strict interpretations of God's law to impose rigid behavioral standards among the common people.

4. E. W. Nicholson, "The Meaning of the Expression ['am ha'aretz] in the Old Testament," *Journal of Semitic Studies* 10 (1965): 59–66.

> ## When Rituals Lead to Rigidity
>
> The *phylacteries* Jesus refers to in Matthew 23 were strips of parchment—or wooden boxes containing the parchment—that the Pharisees wore on their foreheads and their hands (and sometimes on their left arms, in order to place them close to their hearts). These parchments commemorated God's commands in Exodus and Deuteronomy to love Him "with all your heart and with all your soul and with all your strength" (Deut. 6:5; see also Exod. 13:3–16; Deut. 6:4–9; 11:13–21). God wanted His people to remember to keep His commands and fear Him, so He told them, "Fix these words of mine in your hearts and minds; tie them as symbols on your hands and bind them on your foreheads" (Deut. 11:18).
>
> The long tassels Jesus refers to in Matthew 23 were worn by the Pharisees in adherence to Numbers 15:37–40, a passage in which God tells the Israelites to wear tassels with blue cords on the corners of their robes—again with the intent of encouraging them to remember His commands and obey Him. In other words, the tassels and the phylacteries were *symbols* by which God's people were to remember His Word. But instead of humbly committing themselves to reverent remembrance, the Pharisees missed God's point. They got hung up on trying to *look* spiritual. They became consumed with seeing who could strap the biggest, most beautiful box on his head and who could make his fringes the fluffiest!
>
> J. Julius Scott Jr., *Jewish Backgrounds of the New Testament*
(Grand Rapids: Baker Academic, 1995), 251–52

They had vigorous debates about what type of food you could or couldn't eat, how to cut your hair, how to bandage blisters, and when you could or couldn't be physically intimate with your spouse. They were obsessive about religious policy but obtuse about a personal relationship with God, and the oppressive way they enforced unnecessary religious minutiae infuriated Jesus. Instead of demonstrating brokenness and repentance, they epitomized spiritual pride. And on several occasions, He rebuked them for showboating orthodoxy sans compassion. For being great pretenders who didn't practice what they preached. For highlighting their orthodoxy while completely neglecting orthopraxy and orthopathy.

To say that Jesus stepped on their toes with this stinging public rebuke is an epic understatement. The Pharisees weren't just embarrassed by this confrontation; it was the catalyst for them to start planning His murder. And the word He used that likely sparked their entitled religiosity into homicidal rage was *hypocrite*.

Hypocrite is a Greek term found only in the Gospels of Matthew, Mark, and Luke, and our Savior is the only one who speaks it. No one else in the entirety of Holy Writ uses it. *Hypocrite* means "actor," and Jesus used this theatrical expression to accuse the Pharisees of some serious spiritual make-believe!

There's probably no other word that would have been more offensive to the Pharisees' egotistical ears because they had nothing but disdain for *actors*. Theater was a pagan Greek phenomenon—a culture religious Jews viewed as immoral and abhorrent. Yet they were surrounded by it because by the time of Christ, the Greeks had conquered much of the ancient modern world (followed by the Romans, who adopted the Greek/Hellenistic way of life), so their licentious culture had become the norm in most civilized nations, including Israel.

The Greeks and Romans violated the holy laws of Torah in every way, shape, and form. Instead of worshiping Yahweh, the one true God, they practiced *polytheism*, worshiping the numerous "gods" of the Greek pantheon, and threw a pinch of astronomy and astrology into their belief system for good measure. They were moral anarchists whose basic creed was "If it feels good, do it!" And the theater was the centerpiece of their lascivious lifestyle. Many ancient Greek plays featured full nudity, with actors engaging in all kinds of pornographic behavior.

Therefore, when Jesus called the religious leaders of His day hypocrites—*actors!*—I imagine the crowd gasped and those Pharisees sputtered while turning bright red. The Messiah insulted those religious poseurs in the worst possible way. No one had ever dared to speak to them like that before. So why did He?

The Son of God expressed righteous anger toward those Pharisees because their pretentious performance was making a mockery of the gospel. They insisted on following a formula instead of repenting and putting their faith in the forgiveness and mercy of God. Their dangerous game of pious make-believe led others to believe that they could never approach God, much less be loved by Him. I mean, good night, who could possibly check off every single item on a six-hundred-plus-item-long checklist of perfectly righteous behavior?

Their emphasis on legalism missed the point and pointed others in the wrong direction. Their acting skills were admirable, but their doctrine was defective. To keep their fig leaves of religious superiority in place, they established an impossible system of hierarchical hoops for others to jump through. They were much more concerned with *looking* spiritual than they were with *loving* God with all their hearts and *loving* their neighbors as themselves. Their formal theology and their functional theology were a million miles apart.

Leaning into the Shape of Living Water

We got a new dog (our third!) recently because these sweet kids were selling goldendoodles in a Buc-ee's parking lot, and I just couldn't resist, especially after Missy held him and declared, "Mom, I already love him, and he already loves me!" I called our vet on the way home and confessed that I might have been suckered into a wolf with worms.

Thus far, wolf or not, he's the sweetest dog I've ever had—and I love canines as much as I love carbs, so I've had a whole plethora of pups through the years—but he is also *Sir Poops-a-Lot*. And since he's technically Missy's dog, we agreed that the heavy lifting of house-training him should fall on her fourteen-year-old shoulders. She was, of course, very enthusiastic about that arrangement in the Buc-ee's parking lot while begging me to buy him.

However, once she had to start getting up with him at six o'clock every morning, her enthusiasm waned. So much so that recently she flat-out refused to get up for his morning ritual. Which led to an unwanted deposit on a brand-new rug, which led to an animated mother and teenage daughter discussion—bagel notwithstanding—which led to my normally very sweet, very kind, and very respectful kid pitching a small fit and mumbling, "Sometimes I wish you weren't my mom."

"*Sometimes I wish you weren't my mom.*" Goodness gracious, I went through heck and back for years, spent everything I had financially and emotionally, to adopt her from Haiti after her first mama died. I have given that child my entire heart; frankly, I don't think it even resides in my chest anymore. The moment I stepped off an old diesel-spewing bus on a dirt road in a primitive Haitian village in the spring of 2012 and her Aunt Fifi placed her in my arms, I was a goner.

She is my first priority after Jesus every single minute of every single day, and she has the audacity to whine about trading me in for a newer, more lenient parent just because of a little puppy poo? Gee whiz, I hadn't even had my coffee before she hurled that harpoon into the softest part of my soul. Of course, it stung a smidge, but she is, after all, a sleep-deprived teenager in the midst of puberty, which means hordes of uninvited gangs of hormones are racing up and down the streets of her precious self all hours of the day and night. Therefore, I knew she didn't really mean what she said. Which is exactly what she whispered through tears during a long hug a few minutes after the meltdown.

I've made so many parenting mistakes since becoming her second mama eleven years ago, but the one thing I've done relatively well is give my daughter room to grow up. To stretch into everything God has gifted and called her to be. I know I'm pathologically biased, but Missy really is a very kind and very respectful young woman. Given the scarcity and trauma of her early years, it would make sense if she were a disingenuous people pleaser like most abuse survivors who typically struggle with serious abandonment issues. Like I was when I was her age. Instead, by the pure grace of God, Missy is gut-level honest. She doesn't curate her emotions with me because she's learned she doesn't need to present the shiniest version of herself for me to keep her. Her position as my kid is more secure than two pairs of Spanx. She will never *not* be my daughter, and I will always love her.

And that right there is the key to calibrating our Christlikeness . . . to merging our formal theology with our functional theology . . . to assimilating our orthodoxy, orthopraxy, and orthopathy. Our position as God's beloved is *secure*. We can share *everything* with Him—our joy, our tears, our hopes, our dreams, our insecurities, our anger, our fears—we even get to have moments when we shake our tiny, all-too-human fists and complain about His parenting, all in the absolute confidence that He will never leave us or forsake us or stop loving us.

SIX

The Odyssey to Theodicy

> Suffering—pain, humiliation, sickness, and failure—is but a kiss of Jesus. Suffering is a gift of God, a gift that makes us most Christlike. People must not accept suffering as punishment.
>
> Mother Teresa

Remember that high school teacher who told us that the key to public speaking was to imagine everyone in the audience in their underwear? Well, they were dead wrong and perhaps even a tad twisted. I've been gabbing in front of groups for four decades now, and while I still haven't mastered the art of public speaking, I can tell you that it's far more helpful and pleasant to imagine the people I have the undeserved privilege of standing in front of as potential friends instead of half-naked adversaries!

A long time ago I started what is now the ingrained habit of scanning an audience for people whose faces beam with the type of faith David describes in Psalm 34:5—"Those who look to him are radiant; their faces are never covered with shame"—as soon as I step on a platform or stage to begin teaching. And when I actually get the chance to meet one of them afterward, I thank them for being an emotional anchor point who unwittingly helped me stay tied to the purpose of articulating the good news of Jesus Christ.

Although there've been hundreds of shiny saints who've helped me carry the message of the gospel throughout the years, there's one in particular I'll never forget. I was teaching at a retreat on the West Coast, and I found myself almost distracted by an especially radiant woman in the front row. She was beautiful—I wouldn't have been surprised to find out she was a model or a movie star—and looked to be in her thirties. But it wasn't her physical features that were captivating; it was the fact that she appeared almost luminescent as she listened intently to me teaching the Bible.

I was so intrigued by the palpable peace and joy in her countenance that when I had the chance to thank her for her kind "hearing posture" after I finished speaking, I told her I'd never met someone with a sheen that glowed as brightly as hers. Then I said that in my experience, people who wore that type of outward expression usually had incredible testimonies about what God had done in the interior of their lives and I wondered if she wouldn't mind sharing with me how she'd experienced His grace.

She humbly agreed and in a soft-spoken but sure manner explained how she'd married the only boy she'd ever dated when she was very young and unfortunately quickly found out that her publicly friendly sports star of a beau was an angry alcoholic in private. After suffering extreme physical and emotional abuse for years, she finally found the courage to leave him, largely because she was determined to protect their young children from his violent outbursts.

However, while they were separated and the divorce was pending, he still had visitation rights. Not long before the divorce was going to be finalized, along with her being granted sole parenting rights due to the documentation of his ongoing abusive behavior, he defiantly announced that he was taking the kids camping. She didn't feel comfortable letting him take their little ones anywhere, much less by himself into the wilderness. Unfortunately, she didn't yet have the legal option of refusing, so she had to let her two older ones go with him while holding on to the baby whom she insisted was too young to sleep outdoors. Less than twenty-four hours later, policemen came to her home to soberly inform her that her estranged husband had taken her two oldest children into the woods and killed them before turning the gun on himself.

With tears streaming down her face, she described God's sovereign mercy despite her almost unbearable sorrow. She explained how their deaths had been instantaneous and they hadn't had to suffer and how in the early stages of grief she'd clung to the miracle that her baby had been spared. Then she described how several years after that tragic loss, she met and fell in love with her second husband—a godly, gentle man—and how they'd recently had their own baby. She said the evil her ex-husband had perpetrated taught her to put her hope in what was eternal. That through heart-rending loss she'd learned to count every moment with her family and friends as a divine gift. Coming from her

> Those stalwart saints modeled *theodicy* for me long before I learned its official definition in seminary: "a response to the problem of evil in the world that attempts logically, relevantly and consistently to defend God as simultaneously omnipotent, all-loving and just despite the reality of evil."

lips, those didn't sound like pithy platitudes; instead, they sounded like faith that had been forged in the kiln of pain.

The most *believable* believers I've met are those who've waded honestly through woundedness without letting go of God's hand. Those who've trudged through dark nights of the soul only to come out on the other side trusting Him more fully, despite still having questions that will never be answered this side of Glory.

Those stalwart saints modeled *theodicy* for me long before I learned its official definition in seminary: "a response to the problem of evil in the world that attempts logically, relevantly and consistently to defend God as simultaneously omnipotent, all-loving and just despite the reality of evil."[1]

Taking the Plunge

A German philosopher and mathematician named Gottfried Leibniz coined the term *theodicy* almost three hundred years ago by combining two Greek words, *theos*—which

---

1. Stanley J. Grenz, David Guretzki, and Cherith Fee Nordling, *Pocket Dictionary of Theological Terms* (Downers Grove, IL: IVP Academic, 1999), 112–13.

refers to God—and *dikē*—which is the name of the Greek goddess of justice and therefore represents a sense of moral order. Yet while that theological term is a mere three centuries old, people have been trying to reconcile the hard edges of life against the backdrop of a benevolent Creator Redeemer for much, much longer. *If God is such a good God, why is life filled with evil, suffering, and hardship?* is not a remotely modern dilemma.

Historians have discovered texts dating as far back as 403 BC in which ancient philosophers wrestled with the idea of a deity/deities who were indifferent or even hostile when "bad" things happened to "good" people, such as the following poetic lament from "The Protests of the Eloquent Peasant":

> To whom can I speak today?
> There are no righteous;
> The land is left to those who do wrong.
> To whom can I speak today?
> There is lack of an intimate (friend);
> One has recourse to an unknown to complain to him.
> To whom can I speak today?
> There is no one contented of heart;
> That man with whom one went, he no (longer) exists.
> To whom can I speak today?
> I am laden with wretchedness
> For lack of an intimate (friend).
> To whom can I speak today?
> The sin which treads the earth,
> It has no end.[2]

---

2. "The Protests of the Eloquent Peasant," in *The Ancient Near Eastern Texts Relating to the Old Testament* 3rd ed. with supplement, ed. James Bennett Pritchard (Princeton: Princeton University Press, 1969), 407.

And of course, it's not just unbelievers who've questioned how divine providence could be braided with mercy given the prevalence of pain and evil in the world. Even Abraham—the father of our three major world religions, Judaism, Islam, and Christianity—questioned God's absolute goodness when he bargained with Him on behalf of the citizens of Sodom, among whom Abraham assumed were at least fifty "good guys."

> Then Abraham approached him and said: "*Will you sweep away the righteous with the wicked? What if there are fifty righteous people in the city? Will you really sweep it away and not spare the place for the sake of the fifty righteous people in it? Far be it from you to do such a thing—to kill the righteous with the wicked, treating the righteous and the wicked alike. Far be it from you! Will not the Judge of all the earth do right?*"
> The Lord said, "If I find fifty righteous people in the city of Sodom, I will spare the whole place for their sake." (Gen. 18:23–26, emphasis mine)

Then my favorite wimpy-dude-hiding-in-a-winepress-who-eventually-became-a-mighty-warrior-for-God, Gideon, also questioned our Creator's unequivocal goodness when he retorted to the angelic emissary of God sent to encourage him:

> When the angel of the Lord appeared to Gideon, he said, "The Lord is with you, mighty warrior."
> "Pardon me, my lord," Gideon replied, "but if the Lord is with us, why has all this happened to us? Where are all his wonders that our ancestors told us about when they said, 'Did

not the L ORD bring us up out of Egypt?' But now the L ORD has abandoned us and given us into the hand of Midian." (Judg. 6:12–13, emphasis mine)

And this inauspicious list goes on. Moses asked God to blot him out of His divine record book because he couldn't understand how Yahweh could be wholly compassionate and still allow genocide (see Exod. 32:32). Until the latter part of his prophetic ministry, Habakkuk couldn't understand how the wicked were able to prosper and feast on filet mignon while the righteous couldn't pay their electric bills and were reduced to feeding their kids beanie weenies (Hab. 1:2–4, 12–17 . . . mind you, I took the tiniest bit of liberty with the Hebrew here, but it's close to the context of that passage!). And at an especially low point in his life, sweet old Jeremiah had the uncharacteristic chutzpah to press charges against the Creator of the Universe for allowing those who perpetrate evil to thrive (see Jer. 12:1).

But when it comes to stumbling saints who need to be tutored in *theodicy*—on the *vindication of God's absolute goodness and providence in view of the existence of physical and moral evil*—Job is my all-time favorite.

Finding Treasure in Divine Depths

When I was younger, the idea of cozying up to Job and studying his Old Testament story sounded akin to sticking my hand in a blender! However, a few years ago—during the same season I was studying the Hebrew word *asher* and the Greek word *makarios* in Scripture (both of which are often translated as "blessed" in our English Bibles but can also be translated as "happy")—Holy Spirit poked me and encouraged me to peruse that primer on theodicy. Like Abraham, I tried to barter and study Lamentations instead, which seems pensive and melancholy enough to me. But He was insistent, and I've learned the hard way where the path of rebellion leads, so I reluctantly turned the pages of this love story we call the Bible to the book right before Psalms:

> In the land of Uz there lived a man whose name was Job. *This man was blameless and upright*; he feared God and shunned evil. He had seven sons and three daughters, and *he owned seven thousand sheep, three thousand camels, five hundred yoke of oxen and five hundred donkeys, and had a large number of servants.* He was the greatest man among all the people of the East.
>
> His sons used to hold feasts in their homes on their birthdays, and they would invite their three sisters to eat and drink with them. When a period of feasting had run its course, Job would make arrangements for them to be purified. *Early in the morning he would sacrifice a burnt offering for each of them*, thinking, "Perhaps my children have sinned and cursed God in their hearts." *This was Job's regular custom.* (Job 1:1–5, emphasis mine)

There are three super important details in these first few verses. The first is that Job was a *good* guy. The phrase "This man was blameless and upright" comes from two Hebrew words, *tam* and *yashar*, which can also be translated as "guiltless, peaceful, and upright." And while some translations use the word *perfect* to describe Job, he was not without sin, as he confesses in chapter 9—only Jesus can be accurately described as sinless—but he was a really,

> ### A Reward to Suffering
>
> The Book of Job has no interest in praising mystery without restraint. All biblical writers insist that to fear the Lord ultimately leads to abundant life. If this were not so, to fear the Lord would be stupid and masochistic. The book does not disown all forms of retribution; rather, it disowns simplistic, mathematically precise, and instant application of the doctrine of retribution. It categorically rejects any formula that affirms that the righteous always prosper and the wicked are always destroyed. There may be other reasons for suffering; rewards (of blessing or of destruction) may be long delayed; knowledge of God is its own reward.
>
> D. A. Carson, "Job: Mystery and Faith," *Southern Baptist Journal of Theology* 4, no. 2 (2000): 53–54

really good guy! If John the Baptist and Mother Teresa got matched on eHarmony, got married, and had a son, he'd probably turn out to be a lot like Job!

Second, Job and his family enjoyed what could be described as the *good* life. He was extremely wealthy, with extensive farmland, livestock, and a huge staff, so in our modern economy "Job Inc." would be traded on Wall Street, he would be listed among the financially elite in *Forbes*, and he could drive an E-class Mercedes. However, one of my favorite commentators, Mike Mason, describes Job as "*clean* rich" instead of "*filthy* rich,"[3] because later on in this book he uses his considerable wealth to help others. He was a

---

3. Mike Mason, *The Gospel According to Job: An Honest Look at Pain and Doubt from the Life of One Who Lost Everything* (Wheaton, IL: Crossway, 1994), 24.

righteous kind of Robin Hood, minus the shoplifting and dalliance with Maid Marian.

Third, as the rest of this passage illustrates, Job was *doing good*. Based on their rotating banquet schedule, his kids knew how to party, and their daddy knew how to pray. The mention of him rising early to seek God on his family's behalf is a common Hebrew idiom that denotes a conscientious habit, which means praying for them was something Job did consistently. He probably had holes in the knees of his jeans from kneeling all the time and an ichthus bumper sticker on his John Deere!

The bottom line is that Job was a *good guy*, living the *good life*, and doing *good things* with his life. Which is why what happens next kind of makes you want to wave your arms at our divine pitcher and holler, "Foul ball, foul ball!"

> One day the angels came to present themselves before the Lord, and Satan also came with them. The Lord said to Satan, "Where have you come from?"
>
> Satan answered the Lord, "From roaming throughout the earth, going back and forth on it."
>
> Then the Lord said to Satan, "Have you considered my servant Job? There is no one on earth like him; he is blameless and upright, a man who fears God and shuns evil."
>
> "Does Job fear God for nothing?" Satan replied. "Have you not put a hedge around him and his household and everything he has? You have blessed the work of his hands, so that his flocks and herds are spread throughout the land. But now stretch out your hand and strike everything he has, and he will surely curse you to your face."
>
> The Lord said to Satan, "Very well, then, everything he has is in your power, but on the man himself do not lay a finger."

Then Satan went out from the presence of the LORD.

One day when Job's sons and daughters were feasting and drinking wine at the oldest brother's house, a messenger came to Job and said, "The oxen were plowing and the donkeys were grazing nearby, and the Sabeans attacked and made off with them. They put the servants to the sword, and I am the only one who has escaped to tell you!"

While he was still speaking, another messenger came and said, "The fire of God fell from the heavens and burned up the sheep and the servants, and I am the only one who has escaped to tell you!"

While he was still speaking, another messenger came and said, "The Chaldeans formed three raiding parties and swept down on your camels and made off with them. They put the servants to the sword, and I am the only one who has escaped to tell you!"

While he was still speaking, yet another messenger came and said, "Your sons and daughters were feasting and drinking wine at the oldest brother's house, when suddenly a mighty wind swept in from the desert and struck the four corners of the house. It collapsed on them and they are dead, and I am the only one who has escaped to tell you!" (Job 1:6–19)

The first seemingly unfair fact here is that satan (I loathe that evil lizard who is the enemy of our souls, therefore I refuse to capitalize his name; thankfully my publisher and editor allowed me this concession!) is allowed to tag along with the sons of God. Because one would think that a heavenly bouncer could've stopped that lying lizard before he ever got the chance to slither up and have a chat with our Creator! If you despise the dragon as much as I do, you'll be encouraged to know the phrase "also came with them," describing the enemy of mankind in verse 6, is often used in other Hebrew texts to refer to an intruder. That means satan is more nuisance than substance here, and while God *allows* him to participate in the conversation, satan is certainly not equal in power or rank with God. In fact, satan isn't mentioned again in the book of Job after chapter 2, verse 7, so he's pretty much a bit player in this drama.

The second ostensibly undeserved detail is that God allows that evil fallen angel to deal a super-decent guy a super-devastating loss. We live in such a justice-oriented climate that this whole scenario of satan hitting Job below the belt comes across as wildly unjustified and probable grounds for a whopper of a lawsuit! Surely Job didn't *deserve* such discriminatory treatment.

While the idea of *deservedness* may seem logical, it isn't biblical. In fact, flip forward in your Bible an inch or so to Matthew 5:43–45:

> You have heard that it was said, "Love your neighbor and hate your enemy." But I tell you, love your enemies and pray for those who persecute you, that you may be children of your Father in heaven. He causes his sun to rise on the evil and the good, and sends rain on the righteous and the unrighteous.

Here at the tail end of His Sermon on the Mount, Jesus blows the idea of deservedness right out of the water. Now let's flip a few pages over to the right to Luke 13:1–5:

> Now there were some present at that time who told Jesus about the Galileans whose blood Pilate had mixed with

their sacrifices. Jesus answered, "Do you think that these Galileans were worse sinners than all the other Galileans because they suffered this way? I tell you, no! But unless you repent, you too will all perish. Or those eighteen who died when the tower in Siloam fell on them—do you think they were more guilty than all the others living in Jerusalem? I tell you, no! But unless you repent, you too will all perish."

This passage is regarded as one of the "hard sayings" of Jesus because it's difficult to swallow. He once again dispels the myth of deservedness by essentially saying what humanity deserves is death.

Yikers. That'll blow your hard drive, won't it? Because that means no matter how many Bible study blanks we've filled in, how often we volunteer at Vacation Bible School, or how many meals we've served to the homeless, we can't earn one of those immunity sticks like they do on that *Survivor* television show. None of us can be "good enough" to shield ourselves and those we love from suffering. Job proves that good people, including people of faith, can and do experience horrific things according to the permissive will of God yet by no particular fault of their own. In this case Job's faith didn't *prevent* his agony . . . it actually *produced* it. And before you start composing an angry email to me, please reread Job 1:8: "Then the LORD said to Satan, 'Have you considered my servant Job? There is no one on earth like him; he is blameless and upright, a man who fears God and shuns evil.'"

God wasn't *punishing* Job; He was *promoting* Job. *Have you considered My main man, Job, you slithery liar? He's faithful* to the marrow of his bones, you bonehead. *He won't turn away from Me no matter how high you turn up the heat on him!* It almost seems like God has taken up the role as Job's publicist. He doesn't remove His hand of protection, as some have taught. Instead, God holds Job up before satan and launches into a sales pitch. In the economy of God, Job's suffering wasn't a demotion; it was a promotion. An honor. A privilege. The Lord quite literally *handpicked Job* for the honorable position of carrying the weight of pain in much the same way the host country of each Olympics picks the final torchbearer who lights the Olympic flame in the Opening Ceremony.

God chose Job with the foreknowledge that he would carry suffering well. Can you imagine how different our lives would be if we began to view pain as a privilege? A difficult journey that *sometimes* (not all the time, because pain and suffering can also be a result of the Fall and/or consequences of sin) God handpicks us to take because He knows we're strong enough to make the trek and knows His glory will be illuminated through our labor? Changing our perspective and our posture when it comes to pain and suffering—viewing it as an honor instead of dumb luck or degrading, then choosing to focus on God's faithfulness during our trial instead of the trial itself—could change the course of our lives and deeply impact the world around us.

In the economy of God, Job's suffering wasn't a demotion; it was a promotion. An honor. A privilege.

Speaking of postures, Job's initial response to losing his wealth, health, and children is imitable:

> At this, *Job got up and tore his robe and shaved his head. Then he fell to the ground in worship* and said:
>> "Naked I came from my mother's womb,
>>   and naked I will depart.
>> The Lord gave and the Lord has taken away;
>>   may the name of the Lord be praised."
>
> In all this, Job did not sin by charging God with wrongdoing. (Job 1:20–22, emphasis mine)

Shaving one's head and tearing one's clothes were signs of anguish in that culture. Job didn't slap on a happy face in public in a disingenuous attempt to convince others he was okay while dying on the inside. He was authentic in his ache. But at the same time, he *worshiped*. Which means that a broken heart and raised hands are not mutually exclusive for those of us who know the love of God.

Let's not be too quick to put dear Job on a pedestal, though, because while his first response to devastation is admirable, he wobbles on his walk of faith just like we often do and by chapter 19 is whining more than shining:

>> He has alienated my family from me;
>>   my acquaintances are completely estranged from me.
>> My relatives have gone away;
>>   my closest friends have forgotten me.
>> My guests and my female servants count me a foreigner;

> they look on me as on a stranger.
> I summon my servant, but he does not answer,
> though I beg him with my own mouth.
> My breath is offensive to my wife;
> I am loathsome to my own family.
> Even the little boys scorn me;
> when I appear, they ridicule me.
> All my intimate friends detest me;
> those I love have turned against me.
> I am nothing but skin and bones;
> I have escaped only by the skin of my teeth.
>
> Have pity on me, my friends, have pity,
> for the hand of God has struck me. (vv. 13–21)

Now, before you get in the other ditch and throw our buddy Job under the bus, remember, theodicy isn't about *our* immutable goodness in view of pain and evil; it's about *us trusting in God's immutable goodness* despite the existence of pain and evil! And thankfully, after his pity party, that's the posture Job resumes:

> But as for me, I know that *my Redeemer* lives,
> and he will stand upon the earth at last.
> And after my body has decayed,
> yet in my body I will see God!
> I will see him for myself.
> Yes, I will see him with my own eyes.
> I am overwhelmed at the thought! (Job 19:25–27 NLT, emphasis mine)

Job's poignant honesty ushers him to a triumphant epiphany at what seems to be the lowest point of his tragic circumstances. It's evidenced by the Hebrew word Job uses for Redeemer in verse 25, which is *go'al*. Elsewhere in the Old Testament, *go'al* is used to describe a kinsman redeemer, which was usually a close relative who stepped in to rescue someone in their covenant family who was in trouble. It could be the relatively mild emergency of getting over their heads in debt, which the kinsman redeemer would then pay off. Or the major emergency of being sold into slavery, which the kinsman redeemer would then rescue one from. Or a marital emergency, such as the case of the widowed Ruth whose kinsman redeemer was named Boaz. He became her second husband and then they had a little boy named Obed (who's in the direct lineage of Jesus!), thereby rescuing her from both an impoverished existence and childlessness. A kinsman redeemer could also serve as an advocate in the case of a legal emergency, formally taking up the cause and case of whatever relative had gotten themself into a heap of trouble.

What makes Job's use of *go'al* especially interesting here is that in Job 16:9, he called God his adversary, so what this passage indicates is that he needs a Redeemer to take up his cause with his Redeemer. A *go'al* to stand in the gap between him and God. It almost sounds like the spiritual version of "Who's on First," doesn't it? It'd be like me saying, "I need you to be my protector to guard me from *yourself*, who's

---

Theodicy isn't about *our* immutable goodness in view of pain and evil; it's about *us trusting in God's immutable goodness* despite the existence of pain and evil!

---

been bullying me." It's crazy talk! Unless you look down the timeline of redemptive history to Jesus and realize that He's the ultimate Kinsman Redeemer who adjudicated our guilty verdict of sin before God the Father by taking our death penalty upon Himself. Only a perfectly compassionate God would make Himself *go'al squared* so that we can be heard, healed, and saved from *never-ending* sorrow and torment. This pivotal chapter in Job's story is a powerful reminder that the sweetest miracles often grow in the hardest soil and that divine joy often crashes the party when we least expect it.

Job's grasp of *theodicy*—thousands of years before that German math whiz coined the term—is solidified by the end of his inscripturated story as evidenced by his sincere speech at the beginning of chapter 42:

> Then Job replied to the LORD:
>
> > "I know that you can do all things;
> > no purpose of yours can be thwarted.
> > You asked, 'Who is this that obscures my plans
> > without knowledge?'
> > *Surely I spoke of things I did not understand,*
> > *things too wonderful for me to know.*
> > "You said, 'Listen now, and I will speak;
> > I will question you,
> > and you shall answer me.'
> > *My ears had heard of you*
> > *but now my eyes have seen you.*" (vv. 1–5, emphasis mine)

Job's burgeoning belief in God's absolute goodness has rightly echoed down through Judeo-Christian history because of how he praised God's faithfulness *before* God restored his health and wealth and family. Job didn't experience a miraculous reconciliation with his wife—the same one who encouraged him to curse God and die in chapter 2, then added insult to injury by complaining about his breath in chapter 19—before he praised God. Nor did he see the balance in his overdrawn bank account miraculously rise to a number higher than what his net worth was prior to losing everything he owned in chapter 1 before he praised God. And he didn't get a text from his now loving wife reminding him to pick up Pampers and baby formula before he praised God. He praised God *before* he experienced restoration!

While it's heartwarming to read the rest of chapter 42, which details how his health, wealth, and family were restored, I think the most miraculous aspect of Job's story is that getting his life back wasn't a prerequisite for him to plant his trust firmly in the faithfulness of God. He couldn't see around the corner of his circumstances when he exclaimed, "My ears had heard of you, but NOW my eyes have seen YOU!" In other words, *No matter what happens in the future, I'm okay as long as I've got you, God.*

I think the pre-restorative timing of Job's vow of renewed faith is the perfect summary of *theodicy*. Because getting the life we always hoped for isn't the true source of our peace, contentment, and joy . . . it's actually the promise of our Savior's presence in those seasons we *didn't hope for* that gives us unshakable peace, even beyond our understanding . . . it's what brings us deep contentment, even in the midst of chaos . . . and it's how we can radiate genuine joy, even when our eyes are filled with tears of sorrow.

Leaning into the Shape of Living Water

So, why does understanding Job's story at a deeper level and learning to define a multisyllabic theological term like *theodicy* matter? When I was barely hanging on to the knot at the end of my own rope fifteen years ago, I asked myself a similar question. Eventually I came up with two reasons.

1. *Dealing honestly, wisely, and compassionately with human pain and the existence of moral and physical evil is an integral part of our job description as followers of Jesus Christ.* No one gets through this life unscathed. Everyone deals with pain and suffering at some level. All we have to do is scroll down today's newsfeed on our phones for proof because someone lost their child due to a drunk driver today, someone who was voted into public office based on their integrity lied today, some people group is experiencing the devastating violence of war today, and someone will die of hunger today. And that's just scratching the surface of today's trauma index. Therefore, since God's second most important command is for us to love our neighbors as we love ourselves, it behooves us to learn how to better connect with and comfort the saints who are suffering around us.

2. *Pain can be a very effective conduit for God's glory.* As counterintuitive as that might sound, God's glory is often highlighted in the milieu of human hardship. Remember the thirty-three Chilean miners who were trapped underground for sixty-nine days in 2010? An estimated one BILLION people watched the dramatic live television coverage of their rescue. But long before those miners were rescued from what many thought would be their grave 2,300 feet below the surface—about half a mile

underground—nineteen-year-old Jimmy Sanchez sent a letter via a drilled air vent to the surface which read in part, "There are actually thirty-four of us down here because God has never left us."[4]

José Henriquez, who functioned as a lay pastor to his entombed crewmates, later wrote a book called *Miracle in the Mine*, in which he described God's palpable presence in the dark: "We—the miners who were trapped among solid, impenetrable rocks—called on the name of God, and he was with us. He sent his Spirit, who always accompanies us, no matter where we go."[5] He went on to share how one week before they were rescued, they had a worship service during which he presented the gospel to his friends, who'd become like brothers during their grueling, two-month-long ordeal. And when his fellow miners were presented with the opportunity to put their hope in the supernatural compassion of our Kinsman Redeemer—despite the misery of their earthly circumstances—twenty-two of them leaned into the embrace of Jesus Christ for the first time! José Henriquez now refers to the sixty-nine days they were stuck in that South American mine as "God's accident" because he believes God used it to make Himself known. In other words, he now considers being buried alive half a mile underground for two months a sovereign stage on which God's glory was showcased. That's what I would call theodicy personified!

---

4. Jonathan Petersen, "God Has Never Left Us Down Here," *BibleGateway Blog*, November 12, 2015, https://www.biblegateway.com/blog/2015/11/god-has-never-left-us-down-here/.

5. José Henriquez, *Miracle in the Mine: One Man's Story of Strength and Survival in the Chilean Mines* (Grand Rapids: Zondervan, 2011), 143.

SEVEN

Our Family Resemblance

> Everyone who returns from a long and difficult trip is looking for someone waiting for him at the station or the airport. Everyone wants to tell his story and share his moments of pain and exhilaration with someone who stayed home, waiting for him to come back.
>
> Henri Nouwen

One of the first sights we admired when we visited the Dominican Republic recently was a larger-than-life bronze statue honoring the Mirabal sisters, Patria, Minerva, and María Teresa. They're beloved national heroines in their country—where they're commonly called "the Butterflies." And while they're not as well known elsewhere in the world, they did grace the cover of *Time* magazine in 1960 with the headline, "Undermining a Dictator." They were reportedly killed in a car accident on November 25, 1960. However, it was proven that those reports were falsified by a government-controlled newspaper known for spewing propaganda. In reality, they were murdered by the cronies of a cruel dictator named Rafael Trujillo (pronounced true-HEE-yo), who'd taken control of their small Caribbean nation in a violent military coup in the 1930s.

The reason Patria, Minerva, and María Teresa were beaten, strangled to death, shoved into the back of a car, and pushed over a cliff to make it look like an accident is because they had the courage to confront the inhumane atrocities perpetrated by Trujillo (who was also referred to as El Jefe, which means "the chief" or "the boss" in Spanish). They were unlikely revolutionaries, given the fact that they were all well-educated, married women with children, living lives of relative ease in the country, as opposed to idealistic young people who made up the majority of those who publicly opposed El Jefe's evil regime. Yet despite the fact that their wealth and rural residences kept them mostly insulated from Trujillo's maniacal autocracy, these women weren't able to sit idly by in sequestered comfort while El Jefe killed innocent people.

Like when he had an estimated twenty thousand Haitians slaughtered during the Parsley Massacre. Tens of thousands of innocent men, women, and children were savagely murdered in 1937 near the northwest border of the Dominican Republic (DR) and Haiti (the DR and Haiti occupy one single island, Hispaniola, which is part of the Greater Antilles and is the most populous island in the West Indies).

The 224-mile border between the DR and Haiti (which existed mostly on paper when Trujillo took control of the DR) was a permeable place: Kids crossed back and forth to go to school and play, ranchers grazed their cattle on either side of the divide, and Dominicans and Haitians worked together, socialized together, and often intermarried. Therefore, which country had control of the area around the border was ambiguous. And that didn't sit well with the control-obsessed El Jefe.

So he sent the DR's army in to clear the area of Haitians—most of whom were farmers—and when they contested his unscrupulous land grab and fought to keep their homes, farms, and small businesses, he ordered his soldiers to kill everyone in the vicinity. The Dajabón River, which is the natural northwest border between the two nations, was soon filled with so many corpses that had been hacked to death by machetes, witnesses say it ran red for days.[1]

After this unmitigated brutality, Trujillo visited the region and defended the bloodletting with these slanderous, bone-chilling words:

> To the Dominicans who were complaining of the depredations by Haitians living among them thefts of cattle, provisions, fruits, etc., and were thus prevented from enjoying in peace the products of their labor, I have responded, "I will fix this." And we have already begun to remedy the situation.[2]

Missionaries who've lived in the DR for years told me they believe the negative light many Dominicans still view Haitians in can be traced back to the Parsley Massacre

---

[1]. Marlon Bishop and Tatiana Fernandez, "80 Years On, Dominicans and Haitians Revisit Painful Memories of Parsley Massacre," NPR, October 7, 2017, https://www.npr.org/sections/parallels/2017/10/07/555871670/80-years-on-dominicans-and-haitians-revisit-painful-memories-of-parsley-massacre.

[2]. Bishop and Fernandez, "Dominicans and Haitians Revisit Painful Memories."

and the way Trujillo defamed Haitians afterward to defend his actions. Unfortunately, I witnessed the ongoing enmity firsthand when I overheard a few casually conversing about how they thought the Haitians living at the landfill "deserved" poverty because they were filthy, uneducated, and prone to a life of crime. One man told me he thought Haitians were no better than roaches. Of course, when he voiced that vile insult, he didn't know that my daughter is Haitian. It's a wonder I wasn't arrested for punching his lights out.

Taking the Plunge

I'm beyond grateful for brave saints like the Mirabal sisters, who fought for the rights of *all people*—regardless of ethnicity, economic status, gender, or nationality—to be treated with dignity. And their deaths were not in vain either, because their martyrdom fanned the flames of revolution in the DR, and within six months, Trujillo's reign of autocratic terror was overthrown and democracy was ushered in.

When I found out the International Day for the Elimination of Violence against Women was created in honor of the Butterflies and is celebrated on November 25, the day they were killed, I made plans to celebrate it with Missy every year from then on. It's a practical way for me to teach her that despite some people's small-minded bigotry and hard-hearted hatred, she has inherent dignity and inestimable worth as a beloved child of the one true God.

Which is the essence of a theological principle called *imago Dei*, which is rooted in Genesis 1:26–27:

Then God said, "Let us make mankind in our image, in our likeness, so that they may rule over the fish in the sea and the birds in the sky, over the livestock and all the wild animals, and over all the creatures that move along the ground."

> So God created mankind in his own image,
> in the image of God he created them;
> male and female he created them. (emphasis mine)

The term *imago Dei* is Latin, and it means "image of God." This redemptive concept that was courageously and compassionately *practiced* by the Mirabal sisters a half century ago was first *preached* by Irenaeus, the bishop of Lyons, in the second century. Although there has been considerable debate among theologians about the specific application of imago Dei, most agree it means all people contain a diverse collection of godlike qualities that together make up our personhood.[3]

Based on the Hebrew preposition *in* of Genesis 1:26–27, the actual image of God isn't somehow carved or superimposed "within" us—it's more like an internal compass. I began to better understand the truism of imago Dei when one of my seminary professors explained that the historical context of this concept goes back to the ancient practice of kings putting statues of themselves in places where they couldn't physically be to represent their reign and authority.[4] In other words, imago Dei is not a "thing" that's implanted in us; it's the very essence of who we are as people of God.

---

3. Roger Olson, *The Mosaic of Christian Belief*, 2nd ed. (Downers Grove, IL: IVP Academic, 2016), 220.
4. Jim Howard and Don Payne, class syllabus and teaching notes, Biblical and Theological Reflection on the Practice of Ministry, Denver Seminary, July 2019.

This audacious miracle has rightly become a crucial facet of Christian orthodoxy. It underscores how every single human being throughout history has been made in God's image and is therefore inherently valuable and deserving of dignity. In other words, we weren't made to be missed and marginalized, beaten and brutalized, or violated and victimized. We were created to enjoy a vibrant, intimate relationship with God, as well as vibrant, intimate relationships with each other, which together make up the *abundant life* Jesus promised His followers in John 10.

Unfortunately, none of us have been loved *perfectly* by other humans because we're all sinners. Worse still, many of us carry scars due to the abusive behavior of others. Quite frankly, I think much of the angry rhetoric prevalent in modern culture is a reflection of old wounds. People are just flat sick and tired of putting up with exploitation, manipulation, and degradation, whether it came from personal abuse like abandonment and sexual molestation or systemic abuse like misogyny and racism.

I read an article not long ago that was written by a lovely woman I used to know from ministry circles. In it, she explained how being deeply hurt and deceived by other Christians had compelled her to spend several years deconstructing Scripture and that she no longer believes the Bible can be read with certainty, nor does she believe that faith in Jesus Christ is the only way through which humans can be restored to a holy God. Reading her deconstruction narrative grieved me in a similar way that reading about the Parsley Massacre did because the main cause of her individual devastation and their entire village's devastation was the cruelty of fellow humans.

The Starting Point of Doctrine

To be a human being is to be directed toward God. Man is a creature who owes his existence to God, is completely dependent on God, and is primarily responsible to God. This is his or her first and most important relationship. All of man's other relationships are to be seen as dominated and regulated by this one.

To be a human being in the truest sense, therefore, means to love God above all, to trust him and obey him, to pray to him and to thank him. Since man's relatedness to God is his primary relationship, all of his life is to be lived coram Deo—as before the face of God. Man is bound to God as a fish is bound to water. When a fish seeks to be free from the water, it loses both its freedom and its life. When we seek to be "free" from God, we become slaves of sin.

This vertical relationship of man to God is basic to a Christian anthropology, and all anthropologies that deny this relationship must be considered not only un-Christian but anti-Christian. All views of man that do not take their starting-point in the doctrine of creation and that therefore look upon him as an autonomous being who can arrive at what is true and right wholly apart from God or from God's revelation in Scripture are to be rejected as false.

Many years ago, Augustine put it this way: "Thou [God] hast made us for thyself, and our hearts are restless until they find their rest in thee."

Anthony Hoekema, *Created in God's Image* (Grand Rapids: Eerdmans, 1986), 5

I can't help but remember my mother's response when I was a teenager and asked her how an elderly relative who went to church every Sunday and faithfully watched certain preachers on television was able to reconcile their faith with their avowed racism. Mom didn't speak for several minutes, and when she did, there was sadness in her eyes and in her voice. She said, "Honey, some people feel so low about themselves they feel the need to step on others to get themselves up off the ground."

Finding Treasure in Divine Depths

Even though I've been in church since I was in utero and became a Christ follower when I was in kindergarten, it took decades longer for me to believe I had any inherent dignity. I began encouraging people to base their identity in the immutable, unconditional love of God long before I could do the same thing myself. Frankly, I think imago Dei is one of my favorite theological tenets to teach because I'm still working on internalizing what I can conceptualize, so my heart needs to hear it repeated in order to memorize the melody.

Consequently, one of the passages I have on a carousel in my mind is Psalm 139 because it's an epic ode to the immeasurable worth God ascribed to us before we were even born. On days when I fuss at Missy for a minor infraction like decorating her freshly ironed shirt with cream cheese or during weeks when I don't spend enough time

> What a glorious concept to ponder,
> that God knows us completely
> *and* loves us unconditionally.

in prayer because I feel intense pressure to write a new message—or finish a book deadline or create content for a podcast series, so the put-your-head-down-and-get-it-done part of my personality shoves my heart into a corner—I've found much-needed restoration and revival in this song King David sang:

> You have searched me, LORD,
>   and *you know me*. (Ps. 139:1, emphasis mine)

My counselor told me once that the most common lament she hears from clients is, "I just don't feel like anyone *knows the real me*." It's definitely been the underlying theme of my sessions with her—the deep longing I have for others to care enough about me to look past my self-protective facades and see all the broken, ugly pieces of myself I've tried to hide or camouflage and still choose to love me *anyway*. What a glorious concept to ponder, that God knows us completely *and* loves us unconditionally.

The next few stanzas echo that miraculous truth because since our God knows us completely, He knows we'll have a hard time hanging on to the truth regarding His complete comprehension *of us*, much less His incredibly biased opinion *about us*, so He prompted David to expound on the truism:

> You know when I sit and when I rise;
>   you perceive my thoughts from afar.
> You discern my going out and my lying down;
>   *you are familiar with all my ways.*
> Before a word is on my tongue

> you, LORD, know it completely.
> You hem me in behind and before,
>   and you lay your hand upon me.
> *Such knowledge is too wonderful for me,*
>   *too lofty for me to attain.* (vv. 2–6, emphasis mine)

In other words, God totally *gets us*. And while I can relate to that notion being too lofty to wrap my head around, I didn't use to find that concept to be "wonderful." As a teenager and well into my adult years, I assumed that, along with trying to please, appease, or impress everybody else in my life, I also had to be winsome with God. However, because my behavior is so often flawed—the whole bagel-and-bad-word incident keeps coming to mind—I imagined Him furrowing His brows at me with pursed lips and a red pen when I wasn't being personable or well-behaved. Surely, God heaved heavy sighs over my imperfections on a regular basis. Surely, He was forced to grade me on a massive curve and secretly wished He didn't have such slow learners like me in the class of humanity. It took a long time for me to genuinely believe that God didn't send Jesus just to *deliver* me from my sins; He sent Jesus because He *delights* in me. And furthermore, that His delight knows no bounds:

> Where can I go from your Spirit?
>   Where can I flee from your presence?
> If I go up to the heavens, you are there;
>   *if I make my bed in the depths, you are there.*
> If I rise on the wings of the dawn,
>   *if I settle on the far side of the sea,*

> even there your hand will guide me,
>   your right hand will hold me fast.
> If I say, "Surely the darkness will hide me
>   and the light become night around me,"
> even the darkness will not be dark to you;
>   the night will shine like the day,
>   for darkness is as light to you. (vv. 7–12,
>   emphasis mine)

Not long after my parents' very acrimonious divorce was finalized, I got upset about something and began to cry—maybe my sister and I had gotten into a little argument or I'd wrecked my bike; I don't remember the trivial reason for my initial tears, but I do remember that what started as a small sniffle soon turned into heaving sobs of grief—so I ran to my room and crawled under the bed so I could grieve in private because I thought Mom had already been through enough pain and definitely didn't need to deal with mine. About thirty minutes later, I heard her open the back door and call me for dinner because she assumed I was playing outside per usual. I didn't answer her because I was trying to stifle my sobs and get my six-year-old self together. But within a minute or two, I heard her footsteps come down the hall and pause in my doorway. I held my breath, hoping she wouldn't hear me. Instead, she gently asked, "Lisa, honey, are you under the bed?" Everything in me wanted to stay hidden, but Mom had drilled the importance of honesty into us from the time we were toddlers, so I reluctantly murmured, "Yes ma'am."

A few seconds later, the dust ruffle lifted and Mom's face—filled with compassionate concern—appeared. Without saying another word, my well-dressed Southern belle of a mama stretched out on our avocado-green shag carpeting and wedged herself under the bed until she was lying right next to me. Then she reached over and took hold of my hand, and we stayed there amid the dust bunnies and sagging bedsprings until my sobs subsided.

One of my professors at Denver Seminary did his doctoral work on intimacy, and he teaches that empathy begets intimacy. Recognizing someone else's anxiety or vulnerability and caring about it helps facilitate the bond of real relationship. The middle section of Psalm 139 paints a poignant picture of a divine Dad who knows and cares about our anxiety and vulnerability. His affection isn't limited to students who sit at the front of His proverbial class in perfectly pressed uniforms and make straight A's. He cares about the kids who try to make themselves invisible and lovingly wedges Himself into whatever crevice we've found to hide in.

I memorized Psalm 139 when I was in high school and can't count how many times I've recited this supernatural poem of comfort and affirmation since then because there have been many more sobbing-under-the-bed kinds of seasons in my life, even as an adult. Probably more so as an adult, now that I think about it. Anyway, because of how this sacred song has brought me hope when I needed it most, I recently encouraged a group of friends in a home Bible study I've been leading for many years to memorize it too. I even incentivized our group Scripture-memory adventure by promising that I'd buy a fancy meal for anyone who memorized it and was able to recite it within a month. I was pleasantly surprised when our entire group of

Tuesday-morning Bible babes memorized the entire psalm and was almost forced to take out a loan to pay the tab for around fifty fancy meals! However, I wasn't at all surprised that the lyrics many of them teared up over in this heart-affirming poetry were the following:

> For you created my inmost being;
>   you knit me together in my mother's womb.
> *I praise you because I am fearfully and wonderfully made;*
>   *your works are wonderful,*
>   *I know that full well.* (vv. 13–14, emphasis mine)

    Several years ago, I was invited to be a guest at an AA gathering (please note, I've changed the identifying details in this true story out of respect for my friends there and my pledge to honor their anonymity). As is customary at such meetings, a woman stood up and began with the phrase, "Hi, my name's Becky, and I'm an addict." After the rest of the group responded with a hearty, "Hi, Becky!" she shared the happy proclamation, "I was so thankful to be cleaning those tubs today, y'all!" As the rest of her story came tumbling out, it became apparent that the day of the meeting coincided with her first day of employment as a hotel room housekeeper.

    She went on to express how grateful she was to find a full-time job when she'd gotten out of prison after doing time on a drug felony and solicitation conviction. (Many of the women I've met in the addiction recovery program I volunteer with have endured the shame of selling their bodies to get money to pay for the drugs they use to numb the pain of the physical and sexual abuse they experienced when they were little girls—it's one of the most heartbreaking cycles of devolving human dignity I've ever witnessed.)

Then she described how earlier that day, she'd stood up in the hotel bathroom she was cleaning to stretch her tired muscles. And when she did, she caught her own reflection in the mirror. Her voice caught for a second while she was describing her experience, so she took a deep breath to steady herself, then she said with calm confidence, "That's the first time since I was six or seven years old that I looked in a mirror and liked what I saw."

The lyrics David penned in Psalm 139:14–15 aren't about him being preoccupied with his abs in the mirror after a month of keto and working out with a personal trainer. Instead, much like Becky, he's reveling in the fact that because we bear God's thumbprint, we have inherent dignity and inestimable value.

However, as glorious as that divine truth is, I think it's one of the hardest things for our finite minds and oft-insecure hearts to grasp because it's not what so many of us have come to believe about ourselves. Most of the friends I get to hang out with every week at Bible study look like they have it all together. Unlike that stumbling saint at the AA meeting, none of them have been incarcerated. None of them have felt forced to sell their bodies in back alleys. Instead, most of them live in nice homes, drive nice cars, and get their hair and nails done at nice salons. And yet their voices caught in their throats just like Becky's did when they recited the verse about God calling them beautiful. Because true and lasting self-worth doesn't come from affluence or appearance; it comes from trusting that the Creator of the universe thinks we're wonderful even though He's familiar with our worst. And it's not a fleeting thought either . . . God thinks about how wonderful we are *all the time:*

> My frame was not hidden from you
>   when I was made in the secret place,
>   when I was woven together in the depths of the
>   earth.
> Your eyes saw my unformed body;
>   all the days ordained for me were written in your
>   book
>   before one of them came to be.
> *How precious to me are your thoughts, God!*
>   *How vast is the sum of them!*
> *Were I to count them,*
>   *they would outnumber the grains of sand—*
>   when I awake, I am still with you. (vv. 15–18,
>   emphasis mine)

Before our biological dad ever made a pass at our birth mom, God knew there would be an "us." He planned our first breath long before our mother's obstetrician smacked our bare behinds. And regardless of the circumstances surrounding our births—whether we were planned or not, whether our birth, foster, or adoptive parents treated us well or poorly, whether we've been nurtured or not—*we are not mistakes.* God lovingly fashioned every single one of our thirty trillion cells, sculpted every single one of our 206 bones, and painted the exact shade of our eyes and color of our skin. Then He stepped back and said, "Isn't this one wonderful?"

I really like how King David uses an innumerable metaphor to describe God's thoughts about us. Have you ever tried to count sand? A mere fistful would take hours and hours to calculate, so just imagine trying to add up every single teeny, tiny grain from all the oceans, lakes, rivers, deserts, and toddlers' sandpits in the entire world. Even the brilliant math savant Dustin Hoffman portrayed in the movie *Rain Man* wouldn't be able to accomplish that accounting feat. David's gritty simile underscores the reality that we are *always* on God's mind!

But then, just about the time we start leaning back in our lounge chairs, reaching into bags of hot buttered popcorn, and really enjoying this epic imago Dei imagery, Dave throws us a curveball:

> If only you, God, would slay the wicked!
>   Away from me, you who are bloodthirsty!
> They speak of you with evil intent;
>   your adversaries misuse your name.
> Do I not hate those who hate you, LORD,
>   and abhor those who are in rebellion against you?
> I have nothing but hatred for them;
>   I count them my enemies. (vv. 19–22)

Remember how John Calvin described the Psalms as an "anatomy of all parts of the soul"?[5] This abrupt shift in Psalm 139—when David confesses overtly negative feelings about the haters in his community—can also be viewed in a positive light. Because yet again, we're given

---

5. Calvin, *Commentary on Psalms*, xxxvii.

a colorful example of a character in biblical history who didn't curate their emotions for spiritual reasons. *Being serious about our faith is congruent with not being fake about our feelings.* Having a Jesus-shaped life does not mean we have to amputate our messy, all-too-human parts! It just means we bring everything—the good, bad, broken, clean, ugly, arrogant, insecure, and scarred—under the protective, transformative wings of God's grace. And it's from under that merciful canopy that we'll find our souls finally standing up straight and the eyes of our hearts staring intently into the perfectly partial gaze of our Creator:

> Being serious about our faith is congruent with not being fake about our feelings.

> Search me, God, and know my heart;
>   test me and know my anxious thoughts.
> See if there is any offensive way in me,
>   and lead me in the way everlasting. (vv. 23–24, emphasis mine)

This holy hymn ends with David baring his heart before the Lord and asking God to help him. Centuries before a cruel despot named Trujillo gave in to his evil impulses, another king who was also given to selfish and destructive behavior, named King David, humbly acknowledged that he needed to be *under God's authority* to exercise good earthly authority. And whether you're a government leader, an industry executive, a social media influencer, or a stay-at-home mom, we would all do well to scoot further under the umbrella of God's unconditionally loving authority, like the king who killed Goliath when he was a kid. Because all of us make daily decisions that impact other image bearers, be they our employees at work, the people in our neighborhood, the friends we do life with, or the family we live with. And we'll never be able to treat them with the dignity they deserve until we recognize His divine thumbprint in ourselves.

> "Love the Lord your God with all your heart and with all your soul and with all your mind and with all your strength." The second is this: "*Love your neighbor as yourself.*" There is no commandment greater than these. (Mark 12:30–31, emphasis mine)

> Warning: The following section contains a depiction of suicidal thoughts that could possibly be triggering, so please read it at your own discretion, and feel free to skip it if it presses on a bruise in your own heart.

Leaning into the Shape of Living Water

In 1999, a few months before Y2K, my dad gave me a handgun. I demurred because I'm not really the Annie Oakley type, but he was insistent because all the "surely this is the end of times" fearmongering that preceded the turn of the century had him worried about how he could ensure my safety, especially since I lived in a house by myself several states away from him.

Dad had taught me how to shoot a gun when I was little because his property was adjacent to a swamp called

Blackwater Creek in Central Florida, so there were some dangerous critters like snakes, alligators, and the occasional wild boar roaming around. But he further insisted that because it'd been a really long time since I'd shot at tin cans he lined up on a log, I needed to go to a gun range to practice, as well as have one of their instructors review all the pertinent safety precautions with me. I honored his wishes, then locked that pistol up in a biometric safe because I never intended to use it, regardless of what happened when the clock counted down to the year 2000.

Fortunately, nothing happened on Y2K. No one had to barricade themselves in a safe room with stockpiles of food and ammo, because the panicky predictions about worldwide technical meltdowns and societal anarchy proved to be hyperbolic. None of the "super" computers running the stock market or nuclear missile silos or the underwater steel bars that keep us safe from man-eating megalodon sharks—oh, wait, that was just a movie!—crashed. Y2K ended up being an imaginary mountain that petered out into a chagrined molehill of "Goodness gracious, we sure got our drawers all twisted up into an anxious knot about a whole lotta nothing."

However, a few years later, something devastating did upend my little corner of the world. The unexpected loss of two significant relationships in my life, which coincided with a sobering cancer diagnosis (which ended up not being too serious and easily removed), ripped a gaping hole in the safety fence around my heart, causing my sense of security to be decimated. In the span of a few months, I went from feeling like a very blessed woman, surrounded by friends and family, to an abandoned orphan who didn't deserve to be loved by anyone and probably never would be again.

Against all my better judgment, I got a ladder from the shed, climbed up high enough to reach the top shelf in my closet, and felt around in the dark until my fingers discovered the hard edges of that biometric safe. Then I put all ten trembling digits on the electronic keypad that only my prints could unlock, and when the top of the safe sprang open and I saw the gun, what little hope was left in my heart shook its head sadly and left me too.

I reasoned with myself that I was only taking it out of the safe for self-protection. Which was reasonable enough that season because a man who'd been arrested, convicted, and incarcerated for multiple violent crimes against women had recently been paroled and had moved in with his elderly father right down the road from me. The sheriff had even paid me a personal visit to encourage me to leave my home until they could rearrest him on a parole violation because they were sure he would reoffend given the fact that he was a "career criminal" with serious mental issues. But deep down in my heart, I knew I wasn't getting that .38-caliber pistol down purely for self-protection.

I slept with it next to me in bed for several weeks, knowing I probably didn't have it in me to shoot an intruder but wondering if I could ever turn it on myself. I didn't really want to kill myself—I just wasn't sure I had the strength to keep on living anymore. But I also couldn't live with the thought of how badly my friends and family would be hurt if I committed suicide. I was tormented by feelings of guilt and despair and isolation. I was terrified by the thought of getting my heart broken again but couldn't imagine a future without anyone to share it with.

Some nights I'd reach across the bed and pick up the gun, feeling its weight in my hand, thinking how quickly death would come if I put a bullet in it and fired it at a particular spot. Then I'd be flooded with fresh guilt about how I could possibly spend one second imagining something so selfish that would surely traumatize the few people I thought truly loved me. I wasn't sure how to go on living but couldn't figure out how to "go out" without inflicting undeserved pain on the people I care about. And the thought of how my actions might cause someone else to doubt the veracity of God's love was distressing.

Eventually, I gave in to Holy Spirit's prompting to start reciting Psalm 139 in the sorrowful solitude of my dark valley. When I first complied, my voice was weak because I'd turned off my phone and hadn't spoken to anyone in several days. But by the time I got to the midway point of the psalm, my voice had found its strength in the prophetic promise of these ancient lyrics:

> If I say, "Surely the darkness will hide me
> and the light become night around me,"
> even the darkness will not be dark to you;
> the night will shine like the day,
> for darkness is as light to you.
>
> For you created my inmost being;
> you knit me together in my mother's womb.
> I praise you because I am fearfully and wonderfully
> made;
> your works are wonderful,
> I know that full well. (vv. 11–14)

When I found myself in the deepest, darkest pit of my life—one I'd dug myself, thought I deserved to be in, and in which I thought I was all alone—God's presence sustained me. Then when my weary heart finally sensed His nearness and opened its eyes, I saw a ladder that had been leaning against the proverbial wall of my pit the whole time. God loves every single one of us more than we can possibly imagine. We literally bear His image, which means that even at our lowest point, we have inherent dignity and inestimable worth. Hang on to that lifesaving truth with all your might, and may it be the lens through which we see and interact with all His other image bearers too.

EIGHT

Christianity Is More *We* than *Me*

> The only answer, the only hermeneutic of the gospel, is a congregation of men and women who believe it and live by it.
>
> Lesslie Newbigin

I spent most of my forties touring with a Christian women's conference called Women of Faith. Which meant I got to spend twenty or so weekends a year with the same crew of Jesus-loving women, as well as some awesome "men of faith" who were on the production team. We ate what felt like a million meals together backstage in catering (rubbery chicken and wilted salads were mainstays). We got stuck in airports countless times together when our flights were canceled or delayed (most of my friends played cards, but I've never been good at cards, so I tried to coerce them into playing concourse charades to pass the time). And we were collectively *amazed* by God's grace when we got to witness hundreds of women leaning into the waiting embrace of Jesus for the first time—or for the first time in a long time—at every Women of Faith event. Watching other people's faces light up with palpable hope and joy when they realize, *A perfect God like that really does love a hot mess like me*, never gets old! We bonded into a kind of "I've got your back" little road family. Sort of like the circus, only without the wild animals and juggling clowns.

For one unforgettable year while I was touring with WOF, CeCe Winans was adopted into our motley crew because she graciously agreed to be the special musical guest on Friday nights that season. If you've had the privilege and pure joy of hearing CeCe sing, you know she's the GOAT (greatest of all time)! She's been revered for decades in the music industry and is often described as "the first lady of gospel music." Frankly, I think she's so anointed by God that angels stop what they're doing in Glory and listen intently whenever she picks up a microphone!

Anyway, one evening during CeCe's set at an arena in Denver, I was so moved by her worshipful lyrics and the rich sound of her voice that I zipped off my knee-high black boots and hurled them onstage, one after the other. You may or may not know that flinging one's footwear onstage is a common response to an incredible performance in traditional Black churches in America. It's kind of like Motown's version of a standing ovation. Therefore, chucking my Cole Haans toward where CeCe was standing in the spotlight was my way of shooting off a confetti cannon and shouting, *YOU GO, GIRL! That's one of the most awesome songs about Jesus I've ever heard!*

Unfortunately, the security guards in the arena didn't interpret my actions that way, and several rushed toward me in the aftermath of my rowdy boot-toss, assuming I was a potentially dangerous fan who needed to be ejected from the concert. Thankfully, our production team explained to them that I was just an overly enthusiastic member of the platform team and assured them that I wouldn't throw anything else, especially since I'd be teaching the Bible from the same stage the following morning! Of course, CeCe found the whole incident hilarious—she *knew* it was a sign of support that only an ardent admirer or crazy friend would attempt in that particular setting—and we've laughed about it and reenacted it several times since.

When author and theologian Henri Nouwen wrote, "Everyone who returns from a long and difficult trip is looking for someone waiting for him at the station or the airport. Everyone wants to tell his story and share his moments of pain and exhilaration with someone who stayed home, waiting for him to come back,"[1] I'm not sure he had shoe-lobbing in mind, but he does paint a poignant literary picture of the kind of supportive community we're wired for as imago Dei (remember, Saint Augustine described our Creator Redeemer as existing in a perfect community among Himself as God the Father, God the Son, and God the Spirit[2]).

Saint Augustine also wrote about our need to be connected to God *and* each other in his archetypal novel *City of God*, in which he portrays three metaphorical "cities"

1. Henri J. M. Nouwen, *The Wounded Healer: Ministry in Contemporary Society* (New York: Doubleday, 1972), 66.
2. Bird, *Evangelical Theology*, 108–9.

that made up his philosophy, as well as the framework of his eschatology: the City of God, the City of Heaven, and the City of the World. Augustine used those city similes to illustrate how Christian community on this earth is divinely established and how, like painted arrows on the floor of humanity, our relationships with one another point other image bearers to the goodness of God:

> We are commanded to love this Good with all our heart, with all our soul, with all our strength; and to this Good we must be led by those who love us, and to it we must lead those whom we love. Thus are fulfilled those two commands on which "all the Law and the prophets depend": "Thou shalt love the Lord thy God with all thy heart, with all thy soul, and with all thy mind," and "Thou shalt love thy neighbor as thyself." For in order that a man may know how to love himself an end has been established for him to which he is to refer all his action, so that he may attain to bliss. For if a man loves himself, his one wish is to achieve blessedness. Now this end is "to cling to God." Thus, if a man knows how to love himself, the commandment to love his neighbour bids him to do all he can to bring his neighbour to love God. This is the worship of God; this is true religion; this is the right kind of devotion; this is the service which is owed to God alone.[3]

The pretend theological boyfriend who gets the lion's share of my affection and admiration, C. S. Lewis, echoed similar sentiments in his classic book *Mere Christianity*:

---

3. Augustine of Hippo, *City of God*, trans. Henry Bettenson (London: Penguin Books Ltd., 2003), 376.

God can show Himself as He really is only to real men. And that means not simply to men who are individually good, but to men who are united together in a body, loving one another, helping one another, showing Him to one another. For that is what God meant humanity to be like; like players in one band, or organs in one body. Consequently, the one really adequate instrument for learning about God is the whole Christian community, waiting for Him together.[4]

The bottom line of what all three of these brilliant theologians are explaining is that you and I were created for deep connections with other people. For real relationships with friends who are willing to carry us to rooftops, whip out a saw, cut a hole, and then lower us to Jesus when we need healing, like that band of brothers did for their paralyzed friend (see Mark 2:1–5). For real relationships with friends who are willing to sacrifice their own comfort and security for our well-being, like Jonathan did for David even though Jonathan's dad, Saul, harbored murderous jealousy for his buddy Dave (see 1 Sam. 20). For real relationships with friends who are willing to walk alongside us, even when we're not the best company, like the way Ruth stuck by her bitter mother-in-law, Naomi, after both of their husbands died (see Ruth 1:1–18). Deep connections with friends who are relatively safe people means we can count on a community who will cheer *with us* and *for us* (preferably sans shoes, though!). Not because we necessarily deserve it but because they claim us as theirs.

[4]. C. S. Lewis, *Mere Christianity*, C. S. Lewis Signature Classic (London, England: William Collins, 2010), 165.

Taking the Plunge

When late Anglican bishop and theologian Lesslie Newbigin describes the congregation—or community—as a *hermeneutic* (the lens through which we see and understand) of the gospel, he is making the bold claim that deep connections with other people can help us see and understand Jesus more clearly. He goes so far as to assert that Christian community is the *most effective* hermeneutic of the glorious Good News our Savior was crucified for:

> The primary reality of which we have to take account in seeking for a Christian impact on public life is the Christian congregation. How is it possible that the gospel should be credible that people should come to believe that the power which has the last word in human affairs is represented by a man hanging on a cross? . . . The only answer, the only hermeneutic of the gospel, is a congregation of men and women who believe it and live by it.[5]

And whether you agree with every single word of Newbigin's assertion or not, our Old and New Testament canons certainly seem to support his premise. Because the imperatives of Scripture (the verses or passages where God commands us to do something) are only 2 percent singular in nature, which means that *98 percent* of the time when God instructs us to do something, it's in the context of community![6] In other words, Christianity is not exclusively

---

5. Lesslie Newbigin, *The Gospel in a Pluralistic Society* (Grand Rapids: Eerdmans, 1989), 222.

6. Jim Howard and Don Payne, class syllabus and teaching notes, Biblical and Theological Reflection on the Practice of Ministry, Denver Seminary, July 2019.

about individual piety and faithfulness. And while some streams of the church tend to overprivatize following Jesus with language that makes our belief system sound like a solo sport, biblical narrative makes it clear that being a disciple of Christ is much more about *we* than *me*.

I was hesitant about disclosing the fact that I'd slept with a gun during the most difficult season of my life. I don't normally have a problem with transparency. I believe being honest about my shortcomings is a practical way to amplify the divine grace I will need until I'm in heaven. However, typing the word *suicide* gave me pause. I lost someone I loved very much to a self-inflicted gunshot wound, so it's a very personal and painful subject. But after a lot of prayer and reflection, I felt like it was important to share my experience to illustrate how dangerous loneliness can be. Even for committed—albeit mistake-prone—followers of Jesus Christ. At this point in my life, I don't believe vibrant Christian faith and long periods of isolation are congruent.

> Biblical narrative makes it clear that being a disciple of Christ is much more about *we* than *me*.

And when I was healing from that dark night of the soul, the weight of my restoration was too heavy for an individual friend to carry. It took a whole lot of helping hands to gather up all the broken pieces of my heart. I needed a *community* of saints to lean on as I limped back toward emotional wholeness and intimacy with Jesus. Frankly, I think we all do. If you're not convinced about the theological importance of community yet—the *absolute necessity* of being in relationship with each other—please consider the following fifty-nine "each other / one another" imperatives in the New Testament, which collectively prove that being a Christ follower without being in community is pretty much impossible.

1. "Be at peace with each other." (Mark 9:50)
2. "Wash one another's feet." (John 13:14)
3. "Love one another." (John 13:34)
4. "Love one another." (John 13:34; John thought it was so important, he uses the phrase twice in one verse!)
5. "Love one another." (John 13:35)
6. "Love each other." (John 15:12)
7. "Love each other." (John 15:17)
8. "Be devoted to one another in love." (Rom. 12:10)
9. "Honor one another above yourselves." (Rom. 12:10)
10. "Live in harmony with one another." (Rom. 12:16)
11. "Love one another." (Rom. 13:8)
12. "Stop passing judgment on one another." (Rom. 14:13)
13. "Accept one another, then, just as Christ accepted you." (Rom. 15:7)
14. "Instruct one another." (Rom. 15:14)
15. "Greet one another with a holy kiss." (Rom. 16:16)
16. "When you gather to eat, you should all eat together." (1 Cor. 11:33)
17. "Have equal concern for each other." (1 Cor. 12:25)

18. "Greet one another with a holy kiss." (1 Cor. 16:20)
19. "Greet one another with a holy kiss." (2 Cor. 13:12)
20. "Serve one another humbly in love." (Gal. 5:13)
21. "If you bite and devour each other . . . you will be destroyed by each other." (Gal. 5:15)
22. "Let us not become conceited, provoking and envying each other." (Gal. 5:26)
23. "Carry each other's burdens." (Gal. 6:2)
24. "Be patient, bearing with one another in love." (Eph. 4:2)
25. "Be kind and compassionate to one another." (Eph. 4:32)
26. "[Forgive] each other." (Eph. 4:32)
27. "[Speak] to one another with psalms, hymns, and songs from the Spirit." (Eph. 5:19)
28. "Submit to one another out of reverence for Christ." (Eph. 5:21)
29. "In humility value others above yourselves." (Phil. 2:3)
30. "Do not lie to each other." (Col. 3:9)
31. "Bear with each other." (Col. 3:13)
32. "Forgive one another if any of you has a grievance against someone." (Col. 3:13)
33. "Teach . . . one another." (Col. 3:16)
34. "Admonish one another." (Col. 3:16)
35. "Make your love increase and overflow for each other." (1 Thess. 3:12)
36. "Love each other." (1 Thess. 4:9)

37. "Encourage one another." (1 Thess. 4:18)
38. "Encourage one another." (1 Thess. 5:11)
39. "Build each other up." (1 Thess. 5:11)
40. "Encourage one another daily." (Heb. 3:13)
41. "Spur one another on toward love and good deeds." (Heb. 10:24)
42. "[Encourage] one another." (Heb. 10:25)
43. "Do not slander one another." (James 4:11)
44. "Don't grumble against one another." (James 5:9)
45. "Confess your sins to each other." (James 5:16)
46. "Pray for each other." (James 5:16)
47. "Sympathize with each other." (1 Pet. 3:8)
48. "Be tenderhearted [toward one another]." (1 Pet. 3:8)
49. "Love each other deeply." (1 Pet. 4:8)
50. "Offer hospitality to one another without grumbling." (1 Pet. 4:9)
51. "Each of you should use whatever gift you have received to serve others." (1 Pet. 4:10)
52. "Clothe yourselves with humility toward one another." (1 Pet. 5:5)
53. "Greet one another with a kiss of love." (1 Pet. 5:14)
54. "Love one another." (1 John 3:11)
55. "Love one another." (1 John 3:23)
56. "Love one another." (1 John 4:7)
57. "Love one another." (1 John 4:11)
58. "Love one another." (1 John 4:12)
59. "Love one another." (2 John 5)

The longer I stumble along on this journey of faith we call Christianity, the more important the communal context of Scripture is to me because those key fifty-nine principles have often been *embodied* in my life by dear saints who've effectively grabbed a corner of my mat, lugged me to the roof, and lowered me to Jesus. The "body of Christ" is not just a metaphor, y'all, and once you realize that—which typically occurs *after* you need other people's help to tote the weight of your own life during especially difficult seasons!—you'll be glad that in His perfect wisdom, God gave *community* the starring role in the drama of humanity instead of pride or self-sufficiency.

Case in point, not long after Holy Spirit and the community of saints He inspired and equipped pulled me out of my pit of despair, I read a story about a group of American POWs during the Vietnam War that deeply resonated with me. The physical conditions of their imprisonment were horrible—dark, dank, dirty—and they were usually sadistically starved, given just enough water and rice to keep them alive. Many of them endured those horrific circumstances for *years*. Thankfully, most of them hung on to hope and never lost their will to survive through an ingenious method of communicating with each other by tapping messages on the bars or walls of their cells.

Since the normal methods of communication for POWs—whispering back and forth or writing messages on toilet paper with the burnt ends of matchsticks—were easily overheard or intercepted, then severely punished by their North Vietnamese captors, four officers who were briefly held in the same cell devised this unique tap system based on a five-by-five alphabet matrix. Then, when they were separated, they taught it to other American POWs, and soon all of them knew the code. One Vietnam veteran, Ron Bliss, describes the decrepit building he was held captive in as sounding like "a den of runaway woodpeckers!"[7]

One of the most popular acronyms they tapped out to each other was "GBU," which was a universal sign-off. It was shorthand for "God bless you."

I also read a book recently about the ingenuity of human interaction. The author shared physiological facts about how babies are incapable of speech and can only use their larynx for emergencies, not for language.[8] Then she listed scientific documentation about how the sound an infant makes when in distress stimulates other people—including typically non-nurturing types of people—to respond and help them. Even Darwinian researchers have to admit there's something legitimate, if not completely quantifiable, in humans that makes us uniquely created for connection with each other.

Finding Treasure in Divine Depths

According to rabbinic tradition, King David's son Solomon, the third king of Israel, wrote Ecclesiastes when he was an old man. Obviously, I can identify with the fact that it took him a long time to learn this: "By yourself you're unprotected. With a friend you can face the worst. Can you round up a third? A three-stranded rope isn't easily snapped" (Eccles. 4:12 MSG). And I can't help wondering if

---

7. "The Tap Code," PBS, accessed August 9, 2024, https://www.pbs.org/wgbh/americanexperience/features/honor-tap-code/.
8. Jodi Picoult, *Leaving Time* (New York: Ballantine Books, 2014).

he reread some of the Hebrew Scriptures with fresh eyes in his advanced years like I have. Because, goodness gracious, I sure did miss God's shout-out to community for the better part of my life whenever I heard a pastor preach / put me to sleep exegeting Leviticus. Just in case you're tempted to examine the inside of your eyelids, too, when you hear "Leviticus," please pinch yourself because I can guarantee the following passage is anything but boring when you take the time to read it carefully!

> These are the regulations for the fellowship offering anyone may present to the LORD:
> If they offer it as an expression of thankfulness, then along with this thank offering they are to offer thick loaves made without yeast and with olive oil mixed in, thin loaves made without yeast and brushed with oil, and thick loaves of the finest flour well-kneaded and with oil mixed in. Along with their fellowship offering of thanksgiving they are to present an offering with thick loaves of bread made with yeast. They are to bring one of each kind as an offering, a contribution to the LORD; it belongs to the priest who splashes the blood of the fellowship offering against the altar. *The meat of their fellowship offering of thanksgiving must be eaten on the day it is offered; they must leave none of it till morning.* (Lev. 7:11–15, emphasis mine)

So, here's the deal. When God's people wanted to express their gratitude to Him for something He'd blessed them with—a healthy baby, an abundant harvest, etc.—they brought a thanksgiving offering to the priests at the tent of meeting (which is where they worshiped when they were transient in the wilderness) and, later on, to the temple in

Jerusalem (once they were established in the promised land and a permanent place of worship was constructed). The details of such a sacrifice were very specific. They had to bring both leavened and unleavened bread, which meant bread made with and without yeast (think pita and focaccia). And they were also commanded to bring an animal—a sheep, goat, or cow—which would then be butchered, after which the animal's fat and entrails (the liver and kidneys) would be burned on the altar according to the parameters regarding sacrifices (see Exod. 35–40; Lev. 1; 3). Finally, the priest(s) would splash the animal's blood on the altar.[9] Once the sacrifice was complete, the worshiper would share some of the bread and some of the meat with the officiating priest(s) (which was the system God established for the priesthood's physical nourishment—kind of like divine Instacart!), then the worshiper was commanded to eat the rest of the bread and meat before the sun came up the following day.

Now stop and think about that for a minute. According to Google, the average yield of edible meat from an adult lamb is around thirty-five pounds, and from an adult goat, around fifty pounds. An average adult cow yields approximately five *hundred* pounds. That's a whole lot of meat to consume in a few hours! How in the world could one grateful worshiper and his family eat between thirty-five and fifty pounds of mutton or goat, much less five hundred pounds of beef, in one day? They couldn't, and that's the whole point. God established a system through which community

---

9. Gary A. Anderson, "Sacrifice and Sacrificial Offerings: Old Testament," in *The Anchor Yale Bible Dictionary*, ed. David Noel Freedman (New York: Doubleday, 1992), 5:875.

was guaranteed for His people because after every thanksgiving offering, they were forced to have a barbecue and invite everybody in the neighborhood to eat all the leftover bread and meat! Which means Leviticus 7 is essentially a holy party primer!

That's not the only time our heavenly Father required His kids to gather around a communal table either. He intentionally packed His family's calendar with daily, weekly, monthly, and yearly feasts and festivals, including

- the weekly Sabbath (see Exod. 16:23–30; 20:8–11; 31:12–17; Lev. 23:1–3);
- the seventh new moon, or the Feast of Trumpets (see Num. 28:11–15; 29:1–6);
- the sabbatical year (see Exod. 23:10–11; Lev. 25:2–7); and
- the Year of Jubilee (see Lev. 25:8–16; 27:16–25).

Plus, our divine Dad threw three massive, mandatory "pilgrimage" parties—Passover, Pentecost, and the Feast of Tabernacles—in which all Jewish males were required to worship at the same sanctuary[10] (see Exod. 23:14, 17; 34:23; Deut. 16:16–17). All three of these spiritual shindigs were days-long celebrations—usually attended by the entire Jewish family—characterized by joyful singing, socializing, and lots of food.[11] That's why Mary and Joseph made the trek to Jerusalem with Jesus when He was twelve years old

---

10. Paul J. Achtemeier, ed., *Harper's Bible Dictionary*, 1st ed. (San Francisco: Harper & Row, 1985), 305.
11. M. G. Easton, *Illustrated Bible Dictionary and Treasury of Biblical History, Biography, Geography, Doctrine, and Literature* (New York: Harper & Brothers, 1893), 256.

to observe Passover (see Luke 2:41-42). Maybe all that carb consumption is what dulled their senses and caused them to accidentally leave the preteen Savior of the world behind for an entire day until they realized He was missing from their caravan heading back home to Nazareth (see vv. 43-45)!

Communal life continues to be a hallmark of God's people in the New Testament too. The early church was defined by its unity in the book of Acts:

> *They devoted themselves to the apostles' teaching and to fellowship, to the breaking of bread and to prayer.* Everyone was filled with awe at the many wonders and signs performed by the apostles. All the believers were together and had everything in common. They sold property and possessions to give to anyone who had need. Every day they continued to meet together in the temple courts. They broke bread in their homes and ate together with glad and sincere hearts, praising God and enjoying the favor of all the people. And the Lord added to their number daily those who were being saved. (Acts 2:42-47, emphasis mine)

The word *fellowship* in verse 42 is translated from the Greek word *koinōnia*, which means "community" and involves close personal relationship. What an awesome neighborhood to live in! They were relational and caring (they "were together and had everything in common"), devoted to God and each other (they "continued to meet together in the temple courts" and "broke bread in their homes")—plus they were fun to be around (they "ate together with *glad* and sincere hearts").

It's no wonder their church was growing like a weed! What started out as 120 believers at the beginning of Acts (1:15) quickly swelled to over 3,000 following Peter's first public declaration of the gospel message (Acts 2:41). Don't forget that this earliest Petrine speech—fancy seminary term for Peter's first sermon!—was given just a month and a half after he betrayed Jesus outside Gethsemane, because the *Pent* in *Pentecost* refers to the fifty days between Passover and Pentecost. I so appreciate that detail in Peter's and the early church's history because it reminds me that our Savior is so merciful—He forgives our worst sins and can restore even the wobbliest of us into solid ministers of the New Covenant!

Pete's second sermon caused an explosive evangelistic response, and thousands more put their hope in Jesus *while* he was being dragged off to jail (see Acts 4:3–4)! The first Christian church of Acts was an exhilarating place to be! Which was surely fueled by the fact that you didn't have to have all your ducks in a row to be authentically welcomed into that hamlet of hope.

> All the believers were one in heart and mind. No one claimed that any of their possessions was their own, but they shared everything they had. With great *power* the apostles continued to testify to the resurrection of the Lord Jesus. And God's *grace* was so powerfully at work in them all that there were no needy persons among them. For from time to time those who owned land or houses sold them, brought the money from the sales and put it at the apostles' feet, and it was distributed to anyone who had need. (Acts 4:32–35, emphasis mine)

Our spiritual ancestors' communal combination of sacrificial giving and real relationship demonstrated great *power* (from the Greek word *dynamis,* which means "force" or "boldness") and great *grace* (from the Greek word *charis,* which means "unmerited favor"). People who didn't yet know Jesus began paying attention to this interconnected crew who were living out the "love the Lord with all your heart, soul, mind, and strength, and love your neighbor as you love yourself" message of the Messiah.

Furthermore, our social justice–oriented but largely Christian-opposed modern culture could learn a thing or two from those ancient believers because a few chapters later—in Acts 6—an effective system of taking care of the poor and powerless is established *by the church*:

> In those days when the number of disciples was increasing, the Hellenistic Jews among them complained against the Hebraic Jews because their widows were being overlooked in the daily distribution of food. So the Twelve gathered all the disciples together and said, "It would not be right for us to neglect the ministry of the word of God in order to wait on tables. Brothers and sisters, choose seven men from among you who are known to be full of the Spirit and wisdom. We will turn this responsibility over to them and will give our attention to prayer and the ministry of the word." (vv. 1–4)

The fact that the first diaconate was established to alleviate a need that arose in their community regarding the daily food distribution to widows further establishes that the Bible isn't simply data about God or divine parameters through which we prove our spiritual devotion, but His Word stresses *and* strengthens community!

Our Inseverable Bond with Christ

Every member of my body must have a communion with every other member of my body. I say *must*. The question never arises, that I know of, between the members of my body whether they will do so or not. As long as there is life in my frame, every separate portion of my body must have communion with every other portion of it. Here is my finger—I may discolour it with some noxious drug; my head may not approve of the staining of my finger; my head may suggest a thousand ways by which that finger ought to be put through a purgation, and this may be all right and proper; but my head never says, "I will cut off that finger from communion." My tongue speaks loudly against the noxious fluid which has done my finger mischief and has blistered it so as to cause pain to the whole body, yet the head cannot say, "I will have that finger cut off," unless the body is willing to be for ever mutilated and incomplete. Now, it is not possible to mutilate the body of Christ. Christ does not lose his members or cast off parts of his mystical body. And therefore it never ought to enter the head of any Christian man whether or not he shall have communion in spirit with any other Christian, for he cannot do without it: as long as he lives he must have it. This does not check him in boldly denouncing the error into which his brother may have fallen, or in avoiding his intimate acquaintance while he continues to sin; but it does forbid the thought that we can ever really sever any true believer from Christ, or even from us, if we be in Christ Jesus.

C. H. Spurgeon, in *The Metropolitan Tabernacle Pulpit Sermons* (London: Passmore & Alabaster, 1865), 11:4–5, delivered on Sunday morning, January 1, 1865

Leaning into the Shape of Living Water

Around AD 400, a sixteen-year-old boy named Patrick living in what is now known as the northeast coast of England was kidnapped by Celtic pirates who scaled the cliffs of his village in the middle of the night to take young men hostage so they could sell them as slaves back in Ireland. Patrick was eventually bought by a wealthy tribal chief who put him to work herding cattle. While he was enslaved in Ireland, he turned toward God, as he explains in his own words:

> After I had arrived in Ireland, I found myself pasturing flocks daily, and I prayed a number of times each day. More and more the love and fear of God came to me, and faith grew and my spirit was exercised, until I was praying up to a hundred times every day and in the night nearly as often.[12]

Six years after being trafficked, Patrick heard a voice in a dream that instructed him to wake up and walk to the sea, where he'd find a ship waiting to take him back home. So the following morning, he slipped away from his captors, walked for several days, found the ship, talked the sailors into letting him on board, and ultimately returned home to England. He then felt compelled to train for the priesthood and, after finishing his religious studies, was ordained as a bishop. Patrick—by then a respected *man of the cloth*—could've spent the rest of his life in the comfort of home, safely ensconced in an English parish. Instead,

---

12. Quoted in George Hunter, *The Celtic Way of Evangelism* (Nashville: Abingdon Press, 2010), 2.

he sensed God calling him back to Ireland, to the land of his oppressors.

His compassion for the Irish was both remarkable and rare among his peers since the Celts were viewed as barbarians because they were largely illiterate, known to strip naked in battle and howl at the top of their lungs, and often decapitated their enemies. Therefore, Patrick's mission to bring the gospel of Jesus Christ to Ireland was unprecedented and considered foolhardy by most.

Yet instead of being rebuffed or beheaded, he was embraced by his former captors because he spoke their language, engaged them in conversation, told colorful stories, sang Irish ballads, prayed for the sick, mediated conflicts, and on at least one occasion blessed a river so the fishermen could catch more fish! During his twenty-eight years in Ireland, Patrick baptized thousands of Christian converts, planted approximately seven hundred churches, and was likely the first European leader to denounce slavery there. His passion for God and his passion for the Irish and their way of life changed the trajectory of the entire nation. In Ireland today, more than six thousand places contain the grammatical element *cill*, which is the ancient Gaelic word for "church"[13] and a testament to Patrick's transformative influence.

Despite those accomplishments, the Catholic Church has never canonized Patrick as a saint because he ruffled too many ancient feathers when he steadfastly refused the church's repeated orders to force his parishioners to change their way of life and adopt more formal Roman standards

---

13. Hunter, *Celtic Way of Evangelism*, 14.

regarding how they dressed, styled their hair, and worshiped. In short, the religious leaders in Rome wanted Irish believers to tone down their zest for life and behave in a more "civilized" Christian manner. But since those rowdy Irish Christ followers had become his dearest friends and closest companions, Patrick chose to defend their way of life instead of advancing his career. I sure would love to see that jolly old saint's expression on March 17 (the date of his death), when millions of people around the world celebrate St. Patrick's Day despite the stiff upper lips of his long-dead superiors!

Modern theologians point to St. Patrick as a shining example of relational evangelism, but I prefer to describe St. Patrick as a man who was shaped like Jesus, because our Messiah is the first One to model prioritizing relationship. The very heartbeat of His incarnate life and ministry was teaching us that *we belong* in the family of God . . . that there's a seat waiting for us at a never-ending, gourmet food–laden buffet table right next to Him.

NINE

The Score Has Already Been Settled

> This "second coming" of Christ our Bridegroom takes place every day within good men; often and many times, with new graces and gifts, in all those who make themselves ready for it, each according to his power.
>
> John of Ruysbroeck

When I was in high school, my boyfriend and I got caught "parking" by the police, and they went to great lengths to scare the amorousness right out of us. They turned on their sirens and blue lights and bellowed through their PA system thingy for us to put our hands where they could see them. Then two officers slowly got out and sauntered toward our car—all the while blinding us with their high-powered flashlight—made us roll down the fogged-up windows, and then soberly asked to see both of our driver's licenses. After studying us for several terrifying minutes, they began to ask questions about who our parents were, what they did for a living, and how disappointed they'd be if they found out about the "predicament" we currently found ourselves in. Of course, we stammered how our parents would probably be very disappointed—I couldn't help imagining Mom sending me to a juvenile detention center because Miss Patti *does not play* with any type of rebellion or deception. Mere moments before I burst into tears over the utter humiliation of being busted and the dread that my parents would find out about what now felt like a tawdry make-out session, they handed our driver's licenses back to us with a look of stern disapproval. They drove the trauma of that night home by soberly telling us a true story about how another teenage couple had been killed by a mentally ill murderer who caught them parking in an isolated area.

For those of you who are under the age of forty, *parking* is a term we older folks used when we had tight skin and high metabolisms to describe making out in a stationary vehicle. And for those of you who may be wondering how in the world I can remember an event that took place almost forty years ago with such vivid detail, my sharp recall is due to the fact that my boyfriend and I ended up being caught parking by the *very same policemen* about two weeks later. Mind you, all we were doing was kissing the second time too, but when those now-familiar law enforcement officers caught us smooching again, you'd have thought we were Bonnie and Clyde! Goodness gracious, we got in so much trouble I truly thought they were going to haul our hormonal selves off to jail. I can assure you I haven't been caught kissing a boyfriend by the police since then. (If you happen to know a single, Jesus-loving, middle-aged man who has a job, I'd be happy to give him my number. Just kidding. Well, mostly kidding.) Yet I'm still prone to freeze up inwardly and get red blotches on my neck when I see the blue lights or hear the blaring siren of a police car.

Which, from my experience, is the reaction lots of regular folks have when religious leaders start talking about the "end times." I mean, not that we get chastised by the police for giving in to adolescent hormones, but we Christians do tend to get nervous and inwardly splotchy when a street address or phone number includes three sixes in a row, much less when we hear news reports about people getting microchips inserted on the top of their hands as a newfangled form of payment—Lord help us all!

Taking the Plunge

Eschatology is the fifty-dollar theological term that refers to the doctrine of "end times," "latter days," or "last things." In other words, eschatology is the field of study that focuses on the final outworking of God's purposes and activity, as well as our ultimate human destiny. And given the fact that eschatology isn't an exact science, there's a wide variation among doctrinal beliefs based on differing interpretations of prophetic passages in Scripture (which are prominent in books like Isaiah, Jeremiah, Ezekiel, Daniel, and Revelation—but can be found scattered throughout the Bible).

Another relevant—albeit potentially polarizing—term within the study of eschatology is *millennium*, which is based on the following passage in Revelation:

> And I saw an angel coming down out of heaven, having the key to the Abyss and holding in his hand a great chain. *He seized the dragon, that ancient serpent, who is the devil, or Satan, and bound him for a thousand years.* He threw him into the Abyss, and locked and sealed it over him, to keep him from deceiving the nations anymore *until the thousand years were ended.* After that, he must be set free for a short time.
>
> I saw thrones on which were seated those who had been given authority to judge. And I saw the souls of those who had been beheaded because of their testimony about Jesus and because of the word of God. They had not worshiped the beast or its image and had not received its mark on their foreheads or their hands. They came to life and reigned with Christ *a thousand years.* (The rest of the dead did not come to life until *the thousand years were ended.*) This is the first resurrection. Blessed and holy are those who share in the first resurrection. The second death has no power over them, but they will be priests of God and of Christ and will reign with *him for a thousand years.*
>
> When the thousand years are over, Satan will be released from his prison and will go out to deceive the nations in the four corners of the earth—Gog and Magog—and to gather them for battle. In number they are like the sand on the seashore. They marched across the breadth of the earth and surrounded the camp of God's people, the city he loves. But fire came down from heaven and devoured them. And the devil, who deceived them, was thrown into the lake of burning sulfur, where the beast and the false prophet had

been thrown. They will be tormented day and night for ever and ever. (20:1–10, emphasis mine)

Based on this passage, in Christian context the *millennium* typically refers to the "thousand-year" time frame that Christ will reign on the earth before the end of world history. But this is also where the rubber meets the road of dissension because people of faith have vigorously disagreed in their interpretations of John's vision recorded in Revelation 20 pretty much since he wrote it down!

The three most common *macro* eschatological views (among which there are many iterations, and these doctrinal waters are further muddied when the term *millennium* is interchanged with the term *tribulation* because they are not technically interchangeable) that have resulted from differing interpretations of Revelation 20 are:

- *Premillennialism*: This is the doctrinal view that Christ's second coming will occur *before* the millennium, at which time He will rule over the nations for a thousand years until history ends. Although not the only interpretation during the first three centuries of the Christian era, premillennialism was the earliest and most dominant position of the church. It declined during the Constantinian and medieval periods, but it attracted widespread attention once again during the nineteenth century and remains very popular today, especially among Christian fundamentalists and conservative evangelicals worldwide.
- *Postmillennialism*: This is the doctrinal view that Jesus will return *after* the millennial golden age,

when good progressively triumphs over evil because of the spread of the gospel and of Christian influence on society. Scholars are in disagreement regarding its origins, but some of its basic ideas were anticipated early in Christian history.

- *Amillennialism*: This is the doctrinal view that rejects the very idea of a future earthly millennium—a literal thousand-year period in history—and instead interprets John's vision symbolically as Christ's reign from heaven in the present church age. Amillennialism waned in influence with the rise of millennial views in the eighteenth and nineteenth century, but since the latter half of the twentieth century it has been gaining in theological popularity. Among Eastern Orthodox, Roman Catholic, and mainline Protestant denominations, it is probably the most widely held position.

Another thing to ponder in the context of eschatology are the two poles of application: *personal eschatology* (where you go in the end, heaven or hell) and *cosmic eschatology* (what will happen to the world when time as we know it ends).[1] I'm guessing that by now some of you are trembling in dread—not unlike me cowering beside my boyfriend in that 1981 Ford Pinto—nervous there will be a test on this material at some point in the future. So let me encourage you to take a deep breath and relax in light of these much less bewildering biblical truisms: In

---

1. Fred Sanders, "The Doctrine of the Last Things," in *Lexham Survey of Theology*, eds. Mark Ward, Jessica Parks, Brannon Ellis, and Todd Hains (Bellingham, WA: Lexham Press, 2018).

Our Promised Future Glory

The "end times" are a source of endless fascination for many Christians. Charts and graphs and timelines make their way into books and magazines and websites. Predictions come and go, prophets rise and fall, and the world just keeps on spinning.

I've had many a church member ask for a series through the book of "Revelations" (not knowing, I suspect, that the last book of the Bible is a *Revelation*—singular, and that Jesus is the One being revealed, not the specifics of a worldwide calamity reserved for the future). They're not wrong to wonder. After all, studying the end times, what we call "eschatology," is vitally important to the Christian life—not because it satisfies our curiosity but because it spurs us toward faithfulness. We labor in the Lord, knowing our work is not in vain, because the future is assured.

First Corinthians 15 is known to Bible readers as the "resurrection chapter." It's a portion of Scripture in which the apostle Paul lays out the reality of Jesus' resurrection from the dead, connects Jesus' resurrection in the past with Christians' resurrection in the future, and helps us see life and death in light of that resurrection power.

Curiously, after 57 verses of explaining the impact and significance of Jesus' resurrection, the apostle Paul gives a word of instruction: "Therefore, my dear brothers and sisters, be steadfast, immovable, always excelling in the Lord's work, because you know that your labor in the Lord is not in vain" (1 Cor. 15:58 CSB). This chapter, focused so heavily on the end times, comes to a close with a powerful call to excellence in doing the Lord's work. Future glory will make

> sense of present suffering. God's work in the future gives meaning to our work in the present.
>
> What is the future? Jesus wins! Properly understood, studying the end times is not a terrible distraction from our work but a terrific motivation for the tasks the Lord gives us. We do his work, trusting the One who holds the future (and the present).
>
> Trevin Wax, "Foreword," in Dayton Hartman, *Jesus Wins: The Good News of the End Time* (Bellingham, WA: Lexham Press, 2019), xiii–iv

the messy midst of human narrative, Jesus came to earth in incarnate form, the Spirit of the living God was poured out, and after Jesus died on a cross for our sins, He rose from the dead to take His place at the right hand of God the Father, where He now sits enthroned and intercedes on our behalf. Therefore, while eschatology reflects on the "final chapter" of human history, the supernaturally happy ending already took place in the middle of our story. Scary isn't looming around the corner; being reunited with our risen Savior is!

Finding Treasure in Divine Depths

The following passage from Mark's Gospel explains why all Christ followers—regardless of our particular eschatological viewpoints—can have peace regarding the future. Although at first it appears to be the inscripturated version of flashing blue lights and an eardrum-piercing siren, don't panic—I promise it's not nearly as alarming as it initially seems:

As Jesus was leaving the temple, one of his disciples said to him, "Look, Teacher! What massive stones! What magnificent buildings!"

"Do you see all these great buildings?" replied Jesus. "Not one stone here will be left on another; every one will be thrown down."

As Jesus was sitting on the Mount of Olives opposite the temple, Peter, James, John and Andrew asked him privately, "Tell us, when will these things happen? And what will be the sign that they are all about to be fulfilled?"

Jesus said to them: "Watch out that no one deceives you. Many will come in my name, claiming, 'I am he,' and will deceive many. When you hear of wars and rumors of wars, do not be alarmed. Such things must happen, but the end is still to come. Nation will rise against nation, and kingdom against kingdom. There will be earthquakes in various places, and famines." (13:1–8a)

Yikers, talk about buzzkill! Here the disciples are, just sprawled out in the grass, drinking Slurpees, chewing on sunflower seeds, checking their social media feeds, and admiring the architecture of the temple, when Jesus says, "Don't get too comfy, guys, because pretty soon everything you're looking at, including the temple, is going to be nothing but a big pile of rubble. Plus there's going to be global warfare, geological crises, massive food shortages, and you're going to get beat up. You're also going to lose every . . . single . . . one of your Instagram followers and Facebook friends. But don't worry, I'm still going to be in control when all that goes down."

I'm taking a teensy bit of liberty with the original text here in Mark 13, but that's the *gist* of what our Savior said.

He forecast big trouble and colossal changes ahead for His followers, then adds soberly,

These are *the beginning of birth pains*. (v. 8b, emphasis mine)

Even though I had two years to prepare, there were still lots of surprises when I brought Missy home from Haiti, and one of the most enjoyable of those has been being inducted into the wild and wonderful world of curly hair. Of course, I knew that since Missy's hair is super curly, it would require different care and upkeep than mine—which is only a tad curly but has become super chemically dependent as I've aged! However, I was unprepared for the vast array of choices in ethnic shampoo, conditioning, and styling products or for the juggernaut of complete strangers who feel free to share strong opinions regarding my child's hair care—much less *touch* her hair!—in grocery store aisles, airplanes, and on social media. And I was blissfully unaware of how often her hair appointments would be or how long they would take. I didn't know we'd get to spend several hours every week and a half or so in Miss Shardey's salon. Oh, and that's just for her natural braided style—when we switch to box braids in the summer to protect her gorgeous curls from chlorine and salt water, it takes between eight and twelve hours from start to finish!

The good news about these marathon grooming sessions is that Shardey is a friendly, Jesus-loving, funny-story-telling, wisdom-bomb-dropping, curly-haired wizard who's become like an aunt to Missy and a dear friend to me. Which is why I was very concerned a few years ago when Shardey doubled over in pain while braiding Missy's hair. She was seven months pregnant at the time, and even though she's really petite, her belly was alarmingly large, so I thought, *I bet she's further along than her OB predicted.* Then, when normally calm and collected Shardey got down on the floor on all fours and began to groan, I thought, *Uh-oh, I better call 911 or start boiling water or something!* About that time, another, older woman who'd been alerted by all the drama walked up. She observed Shardey's deep-breathing exercise for a minute or two and inserted a few questions between the groans, then after a few minutes declared calmly and decisively, "That baby ain't coming yet. She probably just has *gas*."

Because I never got to experience the extraordinary miracle of pregnancy, I don't know the difference between trapped air, real contractions, or Braxton Hicks. But I was very glad that plainspoken woman did because for a minute there I thought Shardey's baby boy was coming two months early! As foreboding as these verses are at the beginning of Mark 13, the main thing to remember is they are the *beginning* of the birth pains. They're early. The eschatological baby isn't even in the birth canal yet. But then Jesus goes on to describe the intense pain that will accompany the next round of contractions:

> Brother will betray brother to death, and a father his child. Children will rebel against their parents and have them put to death. Everyone will hate you because of me, but the one who stands firm to the end will be saved. (vv. 12–13)

In John 10:10, Jesus said He came to bring us *abundant life*, but He didn't say it would be an *easy* life. As a matter of fact, a few chapters later in John's Gospel, Jesus *promises* there will be trouble—"*In this world you will have trouble. But take heart! I have overcome the world*" (16:33, emphasis mine). So, no matter what your opinion is about what will happen when life as we know it is no more—whether you're a *premillennialist*, a *postmillennialist*, an *amillennialist*, or befuddled by this whole conversation because your only association with the end times comes from the Hunger Games movies, we're all *guaranteed* to go through difficult, sometimes even devastating, seasons in our lifetimes.

However, before you hurl this book across the room and head straight for Dunkin' Donuts, depressed, consider this next passage in Mark with me because tangible hope begins to scooch gloom and doom to the edge of humanity's storyline!

But in those days, following that distress,

> "the sun will be darkened,
>   and the moon will not give its light;
> the stars will fall from the sky,
>   and the heavenly bodies will be shaken."

At that time people will see the Son of Man coming in clouds with great power and glory. And he will send his angels and gather his elect from the four winds, from the ends of the earth to the ends of the heavens. (13:24–27, emphasis mine)

I know, I know—at first glance that sounds about as hopeful as a root canal! It reads kind like the scriptural version of the theme from *Jaws: bah-bum . . . bah-bum . . .*

bah-bum, bum-pum-pum-pum-bum-pum. But there are some hugely revelatory and redemptive nuggets in this passage that change the tune of the text from *Jaws* to *Rocky*!

Reread verses 24–25—the part about a solar eclipse, the moon switching off, and all kinds of shaking going on. Okay, now read the crucifixion account in Matthew:

> From noon until three in the afternoon, *darkness came over the whole land.* About three in the afternoon Jesus cried out with a loud voice, "Elí, Elí, lemá sabachtháni?" that is, "My God, my God, why have you abandoned me?"
>
> When some of those standing there heard this, they said, "He's calling for Elijah."
>
> Immediately one of them ran and got a sponge, filled it with sour wine, put it on a stick, and offered him a drink. But the rest said, "Let's see if Elijah comes to save him."
>
> But Jesus cried out again with a loud voice and gave up his spirit. Suddenly, the curtain of the sanctuary was torn in two from top to bottom, *the earth quaked, and the rocks were split.* (Matt. 27:45–51 CSB, emphasis mine)

Sound familiar? *Total darkness, colossal quaking.* Can you see why many New Testament scholars and theologians point to this passage as proof that Jesus has *already* taken the brunt of this apocalyptic prophecy? He *already* received the wrath of God; He *already* dealt with the darkness that came when God turned His face away from the sinfulness of humanity.

Despite my youthful proclivity for parking, which led to those terribly embarrassing confrontations with officers of the law, I've only had to go to court one time for a speeding ticket. So I don't know what it *feels* like to stand at the defense table before a judge who's about to give me the death penalty. But if you believe the Bible to be true, it says that's the consequence for our sin. For the way we've rebelled against a Holy God. Thankfully, when we consider the prophetic imagery in Mark in tandem with Matthew's description of Good Friday, it points to the God of the universe setting down His gavel, taking off His robe, stepping down from His seat of honor, walking up to the proven guilty defendant of humanity, embracing us warmly, then nudging us to the side and receiving the full punishment of death that we deserve.

Jesus didn't just pardon our sins. HE. TOOK. OUR. PLACE.

And there's more good news. Reread Mark 13:26 about Jesus coming back *in clouds*. Before we go any further, may I remind you that when you filter the perfect Word of God through the imperfect minds and mouths of humans—even well-intentioned, seminary-trained humans—it's bound to be distorted at some level. Well, I got this part of the passage wrong for *years*. I can't tell you how many times I taught on this chapter or on the triumphant second advent scene from Revelation 19 and said things like, "When King Jesus splits the clouds and comes riding through on a white horse," or "When the clouds part, revealing the Prince of Peace in all His glory," but that's not actually how Jesus Himself describes His triumphant return here. He doesn't say, "I'll come back *through* the clouds"; He says, "I'M COMING IN THE CLOUDS" (the English word *in* is translated from the Greek word *en*, which can also be translated "with" or "within").

Which may sound like a picky semantic detail, until we look back at God's promissory, protective, and provisional relationship with His people—our stubborn, rebellious spiritual ancestors the Israelites—in the book of Exodus:

> By day the LORD *went ahead of them in a pillar of cloud to guide them on their way* and by night in a pillar of fire to give them light, so that they could travel by day or night. (13:21, emphasis mine)

> The LORD said to Moses, "*I am going to come to you in a dense cloud*, so that the people will hear me speaking with you and will always put their trust in you." (19:9, emphasis mine)

A little later on in the redemptive history of God's people, we read about another theophanic cloud that filled the temple:

> When the priests withdrew from the Holy Place, *the cloud filled the temple of the* LORD. *And the priests could not perform their service because of the cloud, for the glory of the* LORD *filled his temple.* (1 Kings 8:10–11, emphasis mine)

The bottom line is, in biblical narrative, a cloud is often used as a symbol for, or theophany of, God Himself. The Israelites even gave God's presence in the cloud a Hebrew name: *Shekhinah*, which literally means the "dwelling glory" of Yahweh. Therefore, when we consider the *analogy of Scripture*—another fancy seminary term that simply means using the entirety of God's Word to better understand a passage in God's Word—Mark's prophetic description of Jesus coming with the cloud is kind of like Arnold's promise at the end of *The Terminator*: "I'll be back." Jesus is coming back alright, and He's bringing with Him the all-consuming, all-powerful presence of ALMIGHTY GOD! The Son of the Most High God and the Shekhinah dwelling glory of God are coming back to squash satan and all of his demonic minions like roaches under colossal cowboy boots—evil and wickedness don't stand a chance, y'all!

When the King of all kings comes back *with the cloud*, there will be no more cancer. No more child abuse. No more human trafficking. No more ethnic "cleansing." No more racial profiling. No more political discord. No more divorce. No more pornography. No more ghosting. No more gossiping. No more dying. No more crying.

We don't have to live as victims, because Jesus has already ensured the victory!

Since our Savior knows we're slow to pick up what He's putting down, He graciously follows the imbued promise of the cloud with a fig tree metaphor:

> *Now learn this lesson from the fig tree*: As soon as its twigs get tender and its leaves come out, you know that summer is near. Even so, when you see these things happening, you know that it is near, right at the door. Truly I tell you, this generation will certainly not pass away until all these things have happened. Heaven and earth will pass away, but my words will never pass away. (Mark 13:28–31, emphasis mine)

Israel is an arid country with a mild climate—more like Nevada than North Carolina—which means they don't have a lot of deciduous trees that lose their leaves. I've taken four trips to Israel and traveled all over that beautiful land and know from experience that most trees in Israel—like the olive tree—are evergreens. So Jesus chose a fig tree, one of the few trees in the Middle East that does lose its leaves, to explain that the gloomy, dark days of winter are going to be *so over* when He returns for us, His bride!

> We don't have to live as victims, because Jesus has already ensured the victory!

Before we come up for air from this deep dive, let's clarify one more hugely important detail in this passage. All too often, verse 30 is studied like the spiritual version of a crystal ball. Many sincere Christians through the last two millennia have spent lots of time and energy trying to figure out exactly what time frame Jesus was referring to when He said "this generation" will not pass away until "these things" take place. And because many sincere Christians from our modern era have taken the historical marker of Israel's war of independence in the 1940s or the six-day Arab-Israeli war in 1967 and used those modern conflicts as the context for this passage, they believe the return of Christ will take place within the literal definition of a generation, which is typically somewhere between forty and seventy years. Which means they are convinced the return of Christ will happen in our lifetime. So they've stockpiled food and water and medicine to tide them over through the tribulation.

It is *not* my intention to come across as dismissive, insensitive, or disrespectful to *anyone* who has prepared or currently is preparing for the return of Christ by stockpiling basic necessities. Quite frankly, I used to glance at the chubby koi in the pond at our old house and think, *If it all comes down to it, you guys are gonna sustain Missy and me for a while!* But here's an exegetical detail that will encourage you whether you're a survivalist or a skeptic or just a busy believer who hasn't had a chance to run by Costco yet.

The question that prompted this sober sermon in the first place is in verse 4, when Peter, James, John, and Andrew ask Jesus, "Tell us, when will these things happen?" after He prophesies that the temple whose architecture they've just been admiring is going to be obliterated. They are so startled by His forecast that not one stone will remain standing that they are compelled to ask, "*When? When will these things* happen?" In verse 30, using the exact same Greek term *houtos* for "these things" that His disciples used in verse 4, Jesus declares, "Truly I tell you, this generation will certainly not pass away until all *these things* have happened."

And *those things* did happen; the literal temple the disciples were looking at in Mark 13—the one David designed and his son Solomon built—*was* destroyed before the disciples' generation passed away. Because in AD 70, approximately thirty-five years after Jesus's crucifixion and resurrection, a Roman warlord by the name of Titus, who went on to become an emperor, led troops into Jerusalem and demolished the entire holy city, including the centerpiece of Jewish worship, the temple.

Furthermore, in verse 32, Jesus says, "*But about that day or hour no one knows, not even the angels in heaven, nor the Son,* but only the Father" (emphasis mine). In other words, the Prince of Peace doesn't even know the exact date of His own *parousia* (a term for the second coming of Jesus

Christ)! So it seems incredibly presumptuous to me—if not downright dangerous—for anyone to assert that he or she knows exactly when the rapture will take place when God the Father hadn't told Christ the Son yet during His incarnate ministry.

Leaning into the Shape of Living Water

In 2015, three young American men—Anthony Sadler, Alek Skarlatos, and Spencer Stone—two of whom were soldiers, all of whom were Christians and had been friends since they were boys growing up in Sacramento, boarded the 15:17 Thalys train to Paris. Little did they know that a Moroccan terrorist named Ayoub el-Khazzani—who was carrying a concealed AK-47, a pistol, a box cutter, and enough ammunition to cause significant loss of human life—had also boarded that jam-packed, high-speed French train. Sadler, Skarlatos, and Stone were on vacation that day, simply enjoying life. El-Khazzani was on a mission that same day, with plans to take the lives of five hundred innocent people.

Once everyone was settled on board and the train was hurtling toward the home of the Eiffel Tower, el-Khazzani—who'd been holed up in the bathroom preparing for his homicidal plan—burst out into the aisle and opened fire. There was a struggle to restrain him, which was when Stone, Skarlatos, and Sadler charged the assailant and managed to overpower him, despite the fact that they were unarmed. In the aftermath of their heroic actions, those brave buddies from California received official commendations from both the French and American governments (the French even granted them citizenship!), as well as worldwide press for the way they displayed quick courage in the face of horrible evil and thwarted yet another large-scale, deadly terror attack.[2]

The fact that two of those valiant young men were active members of the United States military at the time of the attempted attack is touted as the main reason they were able to confront and take down a would-be terrorist. Because of their training as soldiers, they were always alert to potential threats. Even while on vacation overseas, they were on guard and therefore saved hundreds of lives because of their vigilance. That's one of the key takeaways from Mark 13—which includes the imperatives to be *on guard* or *alert* or to *keep watch* seven separate times! It's also the appropriate posture for Christ followers as we live in the anticipation of our Redeemer's return.

> Then I heard a loud voice in heaven say:
>
> "Now have come the salvation and the power
>   and the kingdom of our God,
>   and the authority of his Messiah.
> *For the accuser of our brothers and sisters,*
>   *who accuses them before our God day and night,*
>   *has been hurled down.*
> *They triumphed over him*
>   *by the blood of the Lamb*
>   *and by the word of their testimony;*
>   they did not love their lives so much
>   as to shrink from death.

---

2. CBS News, "Americans Hailed as Heroes for Foiling Train Attack," updated August 22, 2015, https://www.cbsnews.com/news/france-americans-heroes-gunman-train-europe/.

> Therefore rejoice, you heavens
> and you who dwell in them!
> *But woe to the earth and the sea,*
> *because the devil has gone down to you!*
> *He is filled with fury,*
> *because he knows that his time is short."* (Rev. 12:10–12, emphasis mine)

That "accuser" of our brothers and sisters in the family of faith (I prefer to call the enemy a dragon) has already been hurled down from heaven. And he is a soon-to-be utterly defeated foe. Because when Jesus came out of the grave that first Easter morning, conquering sin and death, He gave that nasty lizard a lethal wound. Satan has a huge sword sticking out of his scaly chest, which is why he's trying to inflict as much damage as he possibly can now because he *knows* his time is short. The conclusive end to history's battle between good and evil has already been written and *we win*!

But it's not quite time to shoot off the confetti cannons. During this already-but-not-yet chapter of history between the first and second advents—in these latter days when we hold on to the testimonies of former saints and the historical proof of Jesus's incarnate ministry while at the same time hoping for His imminent return—we have to be vigilant so the dragon's tail won't catch us off guard . . . and warn others who are in striking range of his wicked schemes . . . and tend to the wounds of those dear saints who've already been bloodied by the beast. Sometimes being shaped like Jesus looks very much like a soldier who moonlights as a medic.

TEN

The Embodiment of Theology

> "Putting on Christ" . . . is not one among many jobs a Christian has to do; and it is not a sort of special exercise for the top class. It is the whole of Christianity. Christianity offers nothing else at all.
>
> C. S. Lewis

I've heard it said that everyone's an athlete—but not everyone's a good athlete. Of course, "good" depends primarily on context. For instance, I was a good high school athlete. Good enough to earn a volleyball scholarship to college, which in the small town I grew up in was good enough to get my picture in the local paper, thereby earning my mom bragging rights for at least a week or two!

By the end of my first collegiate season, I'd progressed from good to better as a result of hundreds of hours in the gym, running drills, scrimmaging, and playing in tournaments almost every weekend. By the end of my senior year at Troy University, I'd progressed into a pretty good volleyball player at the Division 1 AA level and was even recognized as Player of the Week by our local McDonald's, which earned me an extra-large serving of chicken nuggets and fries. It wasn't the cover of *Sports Illustrated*, but copious amounts of fried poultry parts and potatoes are always a big win in my opinion.

Not long after I graduated from college, my context for the game of volleyball was greatly enlarged when I got invited to play in an exhibition game with a couple of other former collegiate volleyball players. For whatever reason, I was positioned at the net directly across from a very nice, very tall girl who'd been an all-American at the University of Nebraska and was currently on the US National Team (which is usually composed of players who are former or future Olympians).

I don't remember how long it took for the ball to get set to her because I was focused on mirroring her lightning-fast lateral movements in hopes of blocking the ball she was going to attempt to slam onto our side of the court. But when it happened, everything came into hyperfocus. I squatted so deep in preparation to block her attack that my fanny almost kissed the court, then I sprang upward with what felt like the raw power of Michael Jordan executing an aerial 360-degree spin and making a slam dunk. I jumped so high that my hands and forearms soared above the net, effectively creating a flesh wall that would surely be impenetrable, even for an Olympian.

Time seemed to stand still while I hung there watching her left arm whip forward with such velocity that the gleaming white volleyball exploded through my hands and smacked me in the face so hard, I ricocheted backward and slammed flat on my back onto the court. Friends who witnessed our lopsided encounter at the net described it as a rowboat going head-to-head with the *Titanic*. All these years later, I can still remember how tiny white stars danced in front of my dazed eyes and how my gracious, far-superior opponent ducked under the net out of concern for my well-being and helped me up from my pancaked position. I was awed by her athletic ability and her sportsmanship and found myself thinking, *Wow, now that's how this game should be played!*

Much like that encounter with a volleyball phenom raised my view of the game—despite the fact that I was flattened in the process!—there are saints throughout history whose stories can help elevate, elucidate, and encourage both our perception and our praxis of how being shaped like Jesus can change the world around us with the radical kindness of God. The following are a few of my favorites.

Taking the Plunge

Madame Jeanne Guyon

Jeanne Guyon was born in France in 1648 to a wealthy Catholic family. She was prone to sickness as a child and was educated mostly by tutors, who found her to be a voracious reader. She was heavily influenced by the religious piety of her parents and one of her older sisters, who served as an Ursuline nun. From Jeanne Guyon's earliest years she reflected a deep devotion to God.

As a teenager she discovered writings that advocated the devotional practice of inner prayer, which was quite different from the standard set prayers and meditations mandated for devotional practice by the Catholic church her family was entrenched in. In her autobiography, she enthuses about how these "prayers of the heart" made her feel closer to God.[1] Through these personal—sometimes referred to as "mental" prayers—she found fresh grace and deeper intimacy with Jesus than she'd previously known.

Unfortunately, when she was only sixteen years old, her emotionally detached parents arranged for her to be married to Jacques Guyon, Lord du Chesnoy—a mean-spirited man twenty-two years older than her. According to biographers and historians, he was a volatile man as well as unhealthily enmeshed with his foul-tempered mother, and both delighted in tormenting Jeanne. Their consistent persecution, the way they isolated her from others, and the tragic loss of two of their five children compelled her to seek deep solace in Jesus and Bible study. Then, after her husband and mother-in-law cruelly manipulated one of her surviving sons to spy on her to sabotage her devotional practices, she began seeking God through passionate vocalized prayer in the middle of the night while everyone else slept.

Their unhappy marriage lasted twelve years, until Jacques's death. Yet at that point, when she was finally free from the bondage of an abusive marriage, she experienced a dark night of the soul in which she lost her spiritual passion

---

1. *Jeanne Guyon: An Autobiography* (New Kensington, PA: Whitaker House, 1997), 20–21.

and her faith deteriorated into dutiful obligation. It wasn't until several years later that she had a supernatural vision (a frequent occurrence for her during prayer) and was flooded with renewed fervor and joy and exclaimed that her passion for God was more vibrant than ever.

Soon after this spiritual reawakening, Jeanne Guyon joined a group of ascetic Catholics led by a Barnabite monk named François Lacombe. She toured parts of France, Switzerland, and Italy for five years with Lacombe, from 1681 to 1686. Lacombe taught and modeled a meditative style of contemplative prayer and emphasized the cleansing of one's inner life through a passive understanding of surrendering to the will of God, which greatly influenced Madame Guyon.

Following her five-year missionary sojourn with Lacombe, Madame Guyon spent the second half of her life writing and speaking about how to have a more fulfilling spiritual life and deeper intimacy with Jesus. And the emotive, experiential metaphors she used differed significantly from the restrained norm of their day. For instance, she had the courageous audacity to assert that the kiss recorded at the beginning of the Song of Songs—"Let him kiss me with the kisses of his mouth—for your love is more delightful than wine" (1:2)—applied to all Christ followers, not simply Solomon and his bride, whom this biblical poetry is about. She went on to describe *the kisses of his mouth* as "a real, permanent, and lasting experience of God's nature," saying, "The kiss is the union of God's spirit to your spirit."[2] Her unique style and

2. Jeanne Guyon, *The Song of the Bride* (Sargent, GA: SeedSowers Christian Publishing, 1990), 1.

devotion earned her the respect and friendship of Archbishop François Fénelon. Through Fénelon, her spiritual teachings reached and influenced several wealthy and powerful families in French society.

Alas, some very powerful spiritual leaders took offense over her provocative teaching, including Archbishop Bossuet (whom some referred to as the Catholic answer to Martin Luther and whose friendship with Archbishop Fénelon was irreparably damaged over their opposing views regarding Madame Guyon), the bishop of Grenoble, the Jesuits, practitioners of St. Ignatius, and her own brother, Father de la Motte. I do think it's pertinent to note that most of her detractors had taken vows of celibacy, so it's no wonder they thought her exegesis on the erotic poetry of the Song of Songs was blasphemous!

In what many considered to be a brave and honorable response to the overt opposition Madame Guyon experienced, she asked that her writing be examined by a formal religious council (which ended up being composed of the very men who maligned her) and was summarily found guilty of heresy, censured by the pope, and twice held captive. In 1688, she was confined to a convent for several months. Then in December 1695, she was imprisoned in the infamous Bastille. She was released in 1703 and spent the last fifteen years of her life exiled from Paris and French society at the country estate of her son-in-law, but she continued to receive and encourage guests and devotees up until the time of her death. Although she never taught publicly again after leaving the Bastille, her spiritual influence remained significant through the advocacy of Fénelon, followed by spiritual leaders since, such as Thomas Merton,

Witnesses to the Faith

In the judicial procedure outlined in the Old Testament one witness was not adequate for personal testimony against anyone, but two or three witnesses were required (Deut. 17:6; 19:15). This principle was ingrained in Jewish law and is reiterated in the New Testament (cf. Matt. 18:16; 2 Cor. 13:1).

The truth of testimony is so important that the Bible expressly forbids false witness in the ninth commandment (Exod. 20:16; Deut. 5:20; cf. Mark 10:19; Luke 18:20). The practical wisdom of Proverbs speaks out frequently against the false witness (e.g., Prov. 6:19; 14:5; 25:18).

In the New Testament the various words for witness are mainly related to the root *martureō*, "to bear witness, be a witness." The word "martyr" shows the ultimate form of witness in that one may be called upon to lay down his life as a witness to the truth or because of his witness for Jesus Christ.

The followers of Jesus, and particularly the twelve disciples, were witnesses to the person and character of Jesus. They knew him intimately, heard his teachings, and observed his miracles; three were witnesses to his transfiguration (Matt. 17:1, 2; 2 Pet. 1:17, 18) and many were witnesses to his resurrection (Luke 24:48; 1 Cor. 15:4-8). They were specifically commissioned to be his witnesses at the time of his ascension (Acts 1:8), with the promise of the enabling of the Holy Spirit for this work (vv. 4, 8). The Book of Acts is replete with the accounts of that witness of the Holy Spirit through obedient believers.

Walter A. Elwell and Barry J. Beitzel, "Witness," in *Baker Encyclopedia of the Bible* (Grand Rapids: Baker Academic, 1988), 2:2155

A. W. Tozer, John Wesley, Hudson Taylor, and many others. In fact, Watchman Nee (1903–1972)—a Christian writer and evangelist—was so influenced by Guyon's life and writing that he took it upon himself to see that her book *Experiencing the Depths of Jesus Christ* was translated into Chinese and made available to every single convert of "the Little Flock," which is how he referred to Christ followers in the underground revival he was an integral part of in China during the twentieth century. As a result, he was persecuted by his country's communist regime, imprisoned for his faith, and spent the last twenty years of his life in prison.

Thomas Chalmers

Thomas Chalmers was born in 1780 in the small fishing community of Anstruther, Scotland. He grew up in a poor family in which academics were highly valued. Before most children had mastered potty training, wee Master Chalmers's brilliance had bobbed to the surface because, by the age of three, he could read in English, Greek, and Hebrew! And by the age of ten, he'd read every single book in the village where he lived with his mom, dad, and thirteen brothers and sisters!

Long before he started shaving, Thomas Chalmers was packed off to St. Andrews University on the windy east coast of Scotland. (St. Andrews is the village where the game of golf was invented, and its famed golf course has confounded folks swinging clubs at little white balls for centuries. St. Andrews is also the wee hamlet where I took a train from Edinburgh, which is the relatively nearby city where we were vacationing a few years ago, in hopes of running into one of my theological heroes, Dr. N. T. Wright, who was teaching there at the time. But that is a close-to-stalking story I'll save for another book!) There he finished his studies in by-then-predictable record time, earning advanced degrees in mathematics and theology when he was nineteen. By the time he was twenty, he was hired to be both a math professor at St. Andrews and the minister of a small country parish in Kilmany, Scotland, to which he showed more disdain than devotion, as evidenced by an article he wrote in an 1805 pamphlet that said "a minister should be able to complete all his duties in two days and spend the rest of his 'uninterrupted leisure' in whatever manner he wished."[3]

The enormity of young Chalmers's cognitive IQ stood in stark contrast to his underdeveloped heart. Despite his brilliant intellect, his boorish behavior proved he didn't "get" grace. He acted more like a jerk than like Jesus. He came across as arrogant, condescending, and much more interested in *ideas* than *individuals*. Dr. George Grant, an educator and enthusiastic expert on Chalmers who's based here in Tennessee, said this of Chalmers's early life: "He was widely admired but universally disliked!"[4]

Therefore, our compassionate heavenly Father—whom Scripture describes as correcting His kids: "My son, do not despise the LORD's discipline, and do not resent his rebuke,

---

3. Mark Galli and Ted Olsen, "Thomas Chalmers: Unrelenting Advocate for the Poor," in *131 Christians Everyone Should Know* (Nashville: Broadman & Holman Publishers, 2000), 96.

4. Dr. George Grant was a guest professor at Covenant Theological Seminary when I was a student there twenty years ago. (He and his wife, Karen, also attended the same church that I was a member of—Christ Community in Franklin, TN—for a season.) He gave a lecture on Thomas Chalmers with this particular observation, and I wrote it down in a notebook.

because the LORD disciplines those he loves, as a father the son he delights in" (Prov. 3:11–12)—gave Tom a providential time-out. After witnessing the premature deaths of two siblings from tuberculosis, he got really sick too. He was bedridden for months and came close to death's door himself. Yet it was in that weakened physical condition that this gifted young man finally fell in love with His Savior. He realized that in his obsessive quest for knowledge about God and His creation he'd forfeited an intimate relationship with the Lover of his soul. And once he turned his attention to the heavenly Father's unmerited kindness, he became a totally different man.

When he finally recovered his physical health, Chalmers resigned from his distinguished university position to devote his attention and affection to the regular folks in his rural community. He spent three days every week walking the countryside to visit people—whether they attended his church or not. His life became riddled with the language of love.

And while Chalmers had courted fame and political clout as a young man, his relationship with both the British and Scottish governments soured when the courts, against a large church lobby, agreed to continue to let patrons of churches (whether they were members of the Church of Scotland or not) appoint ministers to local parishes (even against the wishes of that particular parish), which was thinly disguised preferentialism in God's house.

That kind of elitist partiality eventually exasperated Chalmers to the point of leading a third of the clergy and members away from the sanctioned, nationally recognized Church of Scotland to form the Free Church of Scotland

(FCS) in 1843 (an event commonly referred to as "the Disruption"). "In a few years, the FCS erected over 800 churches and 500 schools to become the second largest church in the land."[5]

Chalmers worshiped God in sanctuaries and on street corners with passion and practicality. His compassionate sociology reflected his Christ-centered theology. "William Wilberforce, the famous abolitionist, said, 'All the world is wild' about [Chalmers]. And one bishop applied Dante's words to him: 'The holy wrestler, gentle to his own and to his enemies terrible.'" This was because after his conversion, Chalmers "took on a laser-like focus to answer the question he himself once posed rhetorically: 'What is the most effectual method of making Christianity so to bear upon a population as that it shall reach every door and be brought into contact with all families?'"[6]

By the time of his death in 1847, Thomas Chalmers had spearheaded a vast and effective outreach to the poor and underprivileged, planted hundreds of churches, built hundreds of schools, and trained and deployed over eight hundred missionaries to foreign lands. And as if that weren't enough efficacy for God's kingdom purposes, he is also credited with pioneering the Christ-centered "soup kitchen" model, where people in urban areas struggling with poverty and food scarcity receive physical sustenance for their hungry bellies and spiritual sustenance for their hungry hearts. If you've ever had the gift of volunteering at a faith-based outreach that's focused on helping transient, hungry,

---

5. Galli and Olsen, "Thomas Chalmers," 96–97.
6. Galli and Olsen, "Thomas Chalmers," 95.

hope-starved saints, you can thank Thomas Chalmers for it! The second half of his life was beautifully Christoformic, as well as societally redemptive.

Amanda Smith

In 1837, ten years before Chalmers's death in Scotland, Amanda Smith was born in America. Both of her parents, Samuel and Miriam Berry, were born into slavery on adjoining farms in the Baltimore area. Fortunately, Samuel's owners gave him the opportunity to buy himself out of slavery. He toiled night and day for years to "earn" his emancipation and then continued to work tirelessly to pay for the freedom of Miriam and their first five children (who'd also been born into slavery). In all, the Berrys had thirteen children (Amanda was their oldest daughter), and their last eight were born free.

Amanda's parents were devout Christians and well respected in their community. However, despite their emancipated status and good reputation, Amanda and her family still suffered the indignities of low wages, poor housing, scarce access to medical care, and very limited educational opportunities, as the United States was still functioning in a way that severely oppressed ethnic minorities.

Much like Madame Guyon, Amanda married young—at the age of seventeen. However, her marriage was not to a wealthy lord but to an impoverished Baptist minister with an alcohol addiction and anger management issues. They had two children, one of whom died in infancy. It was during the first year of marriage that Amanda fell ill, and the doctor who'd been called in to help confessed there was nothing more he could do for her and that her death was imminent. The following day, while in a deep sleep, she had a vision of an angel encouraging her three times to "go back," as well as a vision of being elevated on a platform between two trees with a large Bible open in front of her as she preached to thousands of people. When she woke up, she was no longer deathly ill and had made up her mind to pray and lead a Christian life, reasoning that God had spared her life for a purpose.

But it wasn't until 1869—after her first husband died in the Civil War, she'd remarried, given birth to (but ultimately lost) three more babies, was widowed again by her second husband, and had what she considered to be her true conversion experience—that Amanda Smith stepped up to the pulpit in an AME church and preached her first sermon. Her spiritual influence blossomed alongside the growth of North American Christianity, which was expanding in the nineteenth century, fueled by its more intimate and eclectic praxis due to the sacrifices of saints like Jeanne Guyon.

But we must remember that much like in Guyon's experience two centuries earlier, most of the theological conversations in Amanda Smith's era were still taking place in atmospheres largely dominated by white males, in which there existed intense opposition to women serving in public ministry or ministry leadership. Which makes the trajectory of her life over the next four and a half decades nothing short of miraculous! She became a Methodist minister, founded the Amanda Smith Orphan's Home for African American Children in Illinois (the first orphanage solely for Black children in that region), and shared the gospel of Jesus Christ on four continents, becoming the first Black woman to be recognized as an international evangelist in

1878. Despite possessing neither a seminary education (she only had three months of formal schooling as a child) nor the relative financial security that most male vocational ministers had at that time, God opened doors for her to preach from platforms that had never before included a woman, much less a woman of color!

Apart from God's intervention, it's highly unlikely that a precious young girl born into slavery could grow up and become an internationally known Christian leader like Amanda Smith did. Yet she didn't rest on her laurels and surely never read her own press because she was dearly loved for her humble dress and speaking style, her powerful, albeit plainspoken prayers, and her habit of bursting into a triumphant song of praise in the middle of a sermon or prayer service until her death in 1915. The world around Amanda Smith was truly transformed by the radical kindness of God, who soaked others with His grace through her guileless conduit of a life.

E. Andrew Harper

My dad, Everett Andrew Harper (who hated his first name and refused to list it on his business cards, and while few ever called him by his preferred middle name, much to his delight my sister named her second son "Andrew" in his honor) experienced his own version of a Damascus Road encounter with Jesus Christ while he was walking the perimeter of his property in a rural part of Central Florida in 1979. Being the owner of forty-two sandy acres that were dotted with scrub oaks and grazed by fifty bored-looking Holstein cows may not sound that impressive, but owning that modest ranch meant the world to my dad. Mostly because when he was a little boy his dad lost their family farm in the wake of the Great Depression. As a result, their family moved from a comfortable life in Knoxville, Tennessee, to a hardscrabble one in West Palm Beach, Florida, where my paternal grandfather took the only job he could find, managing a commercial dairy farm.

Therefore, Dad spent the remainder of his youth getting up at four o'clock in the morning—rain or shine—to help his father milk several hundred cows. Then he'd grab a boiled egg for breakfast, kiss his mama goodbye, and walk several miles to school in shoes with holes in the soles, only to be surrounded by well-heeled peers, many of whom made fun of Dad's material lack. Which is why my relatively small father (he was about 5'7" if he stretched and 180 pounds soaking wet) became such a fierce competitor on the football field and eventually the rodeo, because he channeled his anger into tackling opponents and busting broncs!

Mind you, after practice he had to hustle home, grab a pail, and join his daddy back in the barn to begin the arduous, multi-hour milking process all over again. He told me that during those long, hard years of adolescence, when he felt like a grubby thorn among elegant roses (West Palm Beach is one of the wealthiest cities per capita in the US), he vowed to make a lot of money when he grew up so *his* family would never suffer from poverty like he did. And that desire to reclaim the life his father lost drove my dad down a destructive path for much of his adult life.

He worshiped Jesus publicly on Sunday and most Wednesday nights, too, but during the rest of the week, he worshiped at the altar of commercial success. He pushed himself and those around him hard in a mission to create a small empire that included an insurance firm, a construction crew, and a development company. Dad's intense work ethic and hardnosed style led to marginal business triumphs in his thirties and forties and enough money to buy his beloved ranch and drive new-model trucks around town. However, after a big deal went horribly wrong when I was in high school, he was forced to file bankruptcy and lost everything he owned.

The night before the bank foreclosed on the ranch, he couldn't sleep. He began walking the perimeter of his property, pondering his misfortune. Grieving the fact that he was in midlife—past the energy and earning potential of his youth—and facing the same humiliating ruin that happened to his father. And that's when the Spirit of the Living God dropped my daddy to his knees. Right there on a two-lane dirt road between the Holstein pasture and the Texas Longhorn bull enclosure, Jesus knocked the wind out of his prideful sails. My dad later told me that it was the first and only time he saw a bright light that he believed to be of divine origin.

Dad changed his course dramatically after that night. He said God had given him a second chance to do life right, and instead of being motivated by money, he was going to try and honor Jesus and help others with *whatever* he had. He moved into a little one-bedroom apartment (my stepmother—Dad's third wife—fell in love with the veterinarian at the beginning of his financial downturn and left before he went bankrupt) and began spending all of his free time volunteering at a homeless shelter and teaching Bible studies at the Orlando County Jail. The final three decades of Dad's story were wholly different from the first five.

One of the last coherent requests he made in the days leading up to his death in 2013 was for us to change him into his "good" pajamas and slippers. My sister, mom (she and Dad reconciled during the last year of his life and became dear friends), and I demurred because we were afraid that jostling him in his frail condition would cause too much pain. But he was gruffly insistent. I finally explained our reticence and said, "Daddy, the pajamas you're wearing right now are fine . . . they're clean, I promise." He fixed his blue eyes on mine and croaked firmly, "Lisa, I'm about to be dancing on streets of gold, and I don't want to go up there in old pajamas and bare feet."

Lots of men and women we'd never met—waitresses from the restaurants he frequented, craftsmen he hired straight out of prison when other contractors wouldn't give them a chance, successful businessmen from a monthly men's prayer breakfast he'd gone to for decades, neighbors who were recent immigrants to the US and spoke broken English—came up to us at his funeral to express their condolences and tell us how knowing Dad had changed the course of their lives. They talked about how his passion for God's Word had ignited theirs. How his generosity had inspired them to give more away. How his determination to love others—even when they didn't love him back—for the sake of Jesus was how they hoped to live out the rest of their lives. When Dad died, there wasn't much money in his estate, but my sister and I inherited an invaluable legacy of faith. And while I look more like my sweet mom on the outside, I hope God can see a growing likeness of Dad in my heart.

Finding Treasure in Divine Depths

Missy and I met a sage and sympathetic Messianic rabbi named Samuel several years ago at a live Christmas special taping for TBN. We were all dressed up for the occasion, but despite his elegant attire and the performative nature of a live television set, he was quick to bend down and engage Missy with grandfatherly type questions and then chuckle at her straightforward responses. I'm especially drawn to adults who treat children like they're important instead of like they're interruptions, no matter what setting we're in, so of course I liked him immediately!

During one of our many snippets of conversations when we didn't have to be on camera (he was well-spoken and wise; I was less well-spoken because my Spanx were cutting off the flow of blood to my brain!), he commented about the affectionate bond Missy and I share, then asked if I knew about the contextual significance of adoption in the Bible. I told him that I wasn't sure I did—I mean, maybe a professor covered it in one of my seminary classes, but I couldn't recall it, especially with the whole limited circulation to my cerebral region. He went on to explain how in ancient Jewish culture (as well as most modern orthodox settings), it was legal to disinherit a biological child, but it was illegal to disinherit an adopted child, thereby ensuring that an adopted child couldn't "lose" his or her family.

Please keep that in mind as you read the following greeting Paul gave Christ followers in Ephesus, as well as the fact that this is one of only five times he uses the tender term *adoption* (*huiothesia* in Greek, from the root words *huios*, which means "son," and *tithēmi*, which means "to place") in his epistles (see also Rom. 8:15, 23; 9:4; Gal. 4:5).

> Praise be to the God and Father of our Lord Jesus Christ, who has blessed us in the heavenly realms with every spiritual blessing in Christ. For he chose us in him before the creation of the world to be holy and blameless in his sight. *In love he predestined us for adoption to sonship through Jesus Christ, in accordance with his pleasure and will—to the praise of his glorious grace, which he has freely given us in the One he loves.* In him we have redemption through his blood, the forgiveness of sins, in accordance with the riches of God's grace that he lavished on us. (Eph. 1:3–8, emphasis mine)

My dear friend and mentor, Dr. Lynn Cohick, wrote a commentary on the book of Ephesians a few years ago that quickly became one of the most dog-eared, marked-up tomes in the wall of commentaries I have in my home library. She's recognized throughout modern academic circles as an astute New Testament scholar, but it's not her scholarship that compels me so much as it is the familial relationship between us and God that she highlights in this prison epistle.

Instead of diluting her profundity in my own words, I want to encourage you with an excerpt taken directly from her New International Commentary on the New Testament volume on the letter to the Ephesians:

> The adoption happens through Jesus Christ. The powerful metaphor of adoption deserves a closer look to understand its social context in the first century and its Old Testament context, before turning to the term's theological potency.

Adoption of adult sons was quite common among gentiles in the New Testament era, while adoption of girls or adult females was rare to nonexistent. The purpose of adoption was to secure the family's heritage, including a continuation of honoring the traditional gods and goddesses and managing the family's wealth. The family might adopt a young man whose own father was still living (and gave permission for the adoption) and might adopt a son to inherit over a birth son. Rarely would one adopt an infant, to avoid the great risk that the boy would not grow up to be a worthy adult son. Perhaps the most famous adopted son was Octavian who was adopted by Julius Caesar at age eighteen and was later known as Caesar Augustus, the founder of the Roman Empire. Because Julius Caesar was declared a god posthumously by the Senate, Octavian identified himself as a "son of god" (Latin *divi filius*) on many imperial coins and inscriptions. . . . *Implicit in this model of adoption is the reality that a believer is not simply "saved," but is also a member of God's family.*[7]

And it's from that beloved, secure position as the adopted children of God that Paul encourages us to imitate Him:

Follow God's example, therefore, as dearly loved children and walk in the way of love, just as Christ loved us and gave himself up for us as a fragrant offering and sacrifice to God. (Eph. 5:1–2, emphasis mine)

In other words, the biblical *imperative* (command) to follow God's example and be shaped like Jesus is inextricably

---

7. Lynn H. Cohick, *The Letter to the Ephesians*, New International Commentary on the New Testament (Grand Rapids: Eerdmans, 2020), 97–98, emphasis mine.

linked with the biblical *indicative* (statement of fact) that we are unconditionally loved, cherished, and forever claimed by the familial community of our trinitarian Creator Redeemer. This whole Christoformic ideal begins to sound much more natural and feasible when you consider that as believers we *belong* in God's family, doesn't it?

Leaning into the Shape of Living Water

Jeanne Guyon's spiritual passion was molded by the pain, isolation, and persecution she experienced as a sick little girl, a mistreated young wife, and the mother of several children who died tragically. Thomas Chalmers's palpable humility was forged in the kiln of grief following his siblings' deaths and facing the possibility of his own. Amanda Smith's tenderhearted compassion grew out of the rock-hard soil of bigotry and hatred. And my father's gruff generosity was the direct result of God loosening his grip on a spirit of scarcity. All four had wobbly beginnings and wonderful endings. All four experienced the compassion of Christ when they were trembling in fear, wincing in pain, cowering in shame, or shaken with grief. All four dove deeply into biblical waters as part of their healing regimen. And all four changed the world by reflecting some measure of the radical kindness of God they'd received themselves as His beloved sons and daughters.

When theology is lived out in love, our lives and the lives of other image bearers with whom we get to "do life" will be eternally changed. *Soli Deo gloria.*

Acknowledgments

I would be remiss and frankly just downright rude if I didn't acknowledge the weighty contributions of the following folks: Erin Bruffey Whittington, my ministry director, right-hand woman, and kind Holy Spirit conduit, who very graciously and competently handles a gazillion details on my behalf so that I can spend the bulk of my time studying, writing, and teaching about Jesus. To say I couldn't do what I do without Erin managing the logistics of my life is a huge understatement—I wouldn't trade her for all the chips and queso in the world! I'm also indebted to Lisa Jackson, who's been a dear friend, wise counselor, and long-suffering literary agent for decades. She's an absolute gem. I'm also deeply grateful for my professors in the doctoral program at Denver Seminary. DenSem has been like an oasis for me, where I've been able to drink deeply and experience spiritual renewal that I wasn't even aware my heart was yearning for until it found me. In that same vein, the saints and theologians who've graced us with their wisdom and humility at the Kerygma Summit for the past three years have elucidated and expanded my understanding of God and His Word as well as modeled what it means to live a Jesus-shaped life. They include Dr. Craig Blomberg, Dr. Eva Bleeker, Dr. Dorian Coover-Cox, Dr. Lynn Cohick, Dr. Jim Howard, Dr. Craig Keener, and Dr. Scot McKnight. And last but certainly not least, I will be forever grateful for the incredible crew at Revell and Baker Publishing, namely my editors Rachel McRae and Kristin Adkinson, who threw their considerable expertise and gobs of grace into my little corner of the writing world so as to make what God breathed in my heart these past few years a tangible, hardbound reality.

Lisa Harper

Rarely are the terms *hilarious storyteller* and *theological scholar* used in the same sentence, much less used to describe the same person, but then again, Lisa Harper is anything but stereotypical! She's been lauded as a compelling communicator whose writing and speaking emphasize that accruing knowledge about God pales next to a real and intimate relationship with Jesus. Her style combines sound biblical exposition and exegesis with engaging anecdotes and comedic wit.

Pastor Max Lucado calls Lisa one of the "best Bible tour guides around," and author/actress Priscilla Evans Shirer adds, "Her God-given ability to not merely teach the Word but package it in a way that stirs the heart and calls to action is incomparable. When she speaks, ears perk up!"

Lisa's vocational résumé consists of thirty-plus years of church and para-church ministry leadership, including six years as the director of Focus on the Family's national women's ministry, where she created the popular Renewing the Heart conferences, which were attended by almost two hundred thousand women, as well as a decade of touring with Women of Faith, where she spoke to over a million women about the unconditional love of God. Her academic résumé includes a master of theological studies from Covenant

Seminary, and she recently completed her doctoral studies at Denver Seminary and is now working on her thesis.

She's been featured on numerous television and radio programs and is a regular on TBN's globally syndicated *Better Together* show, as well as host of *Lisa Harper's Back Porch Theology* podcast on AccessMore. She's spoken at hundreds of national and international women's events, as well as in churches around the world. She's also invested locally and has been leading the same weekly neighborhood Bible study for fifteen years. And if you can't find her teaching, studying, hiking, or practicing wave-riding skills, she's probably in a coffee shop sipping a mocha and typing away on her computer because she's also had sixteen books published, including the recent bestselling devotional *Jesus*, and has written and filmed eight well-received Bible study video curriculums, including *Job: A Story of Unlikely Joy* and *How Much More: Discovering God's Extravagant Love in Unexpected Places*.

However, when asked about her credentials, the most noticeable thing about Lisa Harper is her authenticity. During a recent interview she said, "I'm so grateful for the opportunities God's given me, but don't forget, He often uses donkeys and rocks!" She went on to describe her greatest accomplishment to date as getting to become Missy's mom through the miracle of adoption. In 2014, after a difficult journey and several adoption losses, she finally got to bring her daughter home from Haiti, and she's been smiling even wider ever since.

CONNECT WITH LISA

LisaHarper.org

@LisaDHarper @LisaDHarper

A Note from the Publisher

Dear Reader,

Thank you for selecting a Revell book! We're so happy to be part of your life through this work.

Revell's mission is to publish books that offer hope and help for meeting life's challenges, and that bring comfort and inspiration. We know that the right words at the right time can make all the difference; it is our goal with every title to provide just the words you need.

We believe in building lasting relationships with readers, and we'd love to get to know you better. If you have any feedback, questions, or just want to chat about your experience reading this book, please email us directly at publisher@revellbooks.com. Your insights are incredibly important to us, and it would be our pleasure to hear how we can better serve you.

We look forward to hearing from you and having the chance to enhance your experience with Revell Books.

The Publishing Team at Revell Books
A Division of Baker Publishing Group
publisher@revellbooks.com

Revell